PRO Readers' Guide No 8

RAF Records in the PRO

by

Simon Fowler
Peter Elliott
Roy Conyers Nesbit
Christina Goulter

PRO Publications

PRO Publications

Public Record Office
Chancery Lane
London WC2A 1LR

ISBN 1 873162 14 6

Acknowledgements

The authors wish to thank the following: Marion Edwards, Jim Murray, Fiona Prothero, and Melvyn Stainton of the Public Record Office publishing team; Ernest Schofield for his assistance with Section Three; Alfred Knightbridge as series editor; and Oliver Hoare, who undertook the picture research. They also acknowledge the valuable help and advice passed between themselves.

CONTENTS

List of illustrations

Introduction

"Why" said the Dodo, "the best way to understand it is to do it" - Lewis Carroll,
Alice In Wonderland

Research into the activities of the Royal Air Force and its predecessors - the Royal Flying Corps, the Royal Naval Air Service, the Air Battalion of the Royal Engineers and the Balloon Section of the Royal Engineers - attracts many visitors to the Public Record Office (PRO) at Ruskin Avenue in Kew. A multitude of relevant documents is available about these activities, and to these must be added the Fleet Air Arm, as well as the records of the Commonwealth Squadrons in the Second World War.

As with all the documents in the PRO, such records normally become available for public scrutiny when they are thirty years old, although a few which are considered to contain sensitive material are closed for longer periods. Many of these documents are available in their original form but some, such as Squadron Operations Record Books during the Second World War, have been transferred to microfilm to prevent further deterioration during handling and usage.

There has to be high security for such a valuable collection of records, and procedures at Kew are firm but courteous and reasonably informal. A newcomer should carry some form of identification, including a passport if not a British citizen. You will then be issued a reader's ticket which includes an identification number which is used when ordering documents. Only a minimum of personal belongings are permitted in the reading rooms, and there is a security check on both entry and exit. Only **pencils** may be used for taking notes.

The first problem to be resolved by researchers is to ascertain the reference letters and numbers of the documents they wish to consult, before ordering these on one of the computer terminals. Each document reference consists of three parts. The first is the 'lettercode', such as AIR. The second is the 'class number', such as 27 for Squadron Operations Record Books. The third is the 'piece number' for the particular unit or record for the relevant period. Thus the Operations Record Book for Scampton, the RAF station from which the Lancasters of 617 Squadron flew on the famous Dam-busting operation of 16/17 May 1943, has the reference AIR 28/682. If this reference is tapped into one of the computer terminals in the Reference Room, together with your identification number and seat number you will be allocated in the Reading Room, the document should become available about twenty minutes later. Only three documents may be ordered and consulted at any one time. Those records on microfilm are found in drawers in the Microfilm Room, if not already in use by other readers.

To enable researchers to trace documents, the reference classifications have been tabulated in bound volumes known as 'class lists'. Two sets of these can be found in the Reference Room on the first floor, with an additional set in the Lobby outside and another set in the Map Room on the second floor. The volumes are lettered from AB 1 to ZSPC 11 on their spines, and most of the RAF references can be found in AIR [Air Ministry] or AVIA [Aviation] lettercodes, but others are in ADM [Admiralty], CAB [Cabinet], HO [Home Office], MUN [Munitions] or WO [War Office] lists.

The class lists contain brief descriptions of the contents of the records, providing signposts which can lead you to the documents containing the information being sought. They are in frequent use by readers and should not be taken out of the rooms in which they are housed but replaced in the correct order on the shelves after use.

There are 74 classes within both the AIR and AVIA lettercodes. A brief description of their contents can be found in the Public Record Office *Current Guide*, copies of which are available at the PRO. Part One of that guide consists of administrative histories of departments, including the Air Ministry, while Part Two contains brief descriptions of all the classes in lettercodes, also including the Air Ministry. Part Three is an index to the other two parts. However, experience indicates that this additional guide, specifically devoted to RAF records, is required.

The RAF records at the PRO constitute a detailed history of the development of the air service, so that much of this guide follows an historical format with particular subjects highlighted as they emerge. Four distinct phases can be recognised in the development of the RAF, and these have been adopted in preparing this guide. The balance between historical analysis and exposition of subject matter varies with the different events in the periods under review.

The first period extends to the end of the First World War, and this section has been written by Simon Fowler of the PRO. The second period, between the wars, has been covered by Peter Elliott of the RAF Museum. There was a vast increase in RAF activities during the Second World War, and these have been dealt with by the author Roy Conyers Nesbit in the third and longest section. The section on the post-war period up to 1963 has been written by Christina Goulter of the Air Historical Branch of the Ministry of Defence. The four authors would like to acknowledge the help given to them by Ernest Schofield, who served in the RAF in the Second World War and has had experience of research in this subject.

The four sections have been written in somewhat different styles. This is partly attributable to the different expertise of the authors but is mainly the result of the changing activities and developments in the air service during the total period. War and peace gave rise to different records, while the RAF itself underwent phases of expansion and contraction over the years.

The techniques to be adopted by researchers will also vary according to the type of project being undertaken. RAF planning required correspondence with outside bodies, both civilian and military, as well as within the RAF itself. Minutes were kept of discussions and decisions were recorded. Instructions were given for work to be done and reports were made about implementation. These matters should be taken into account when searching for the information you require, and it is hoped that the explanations given about RAF activities in this guide might provide pointers for further exploration.

The four authors are unable to provide an answering service for readers requiring further information. However, if you cannot carry out your own research, the PRO is able to provide a list of independent researchers specialising in the RAF who can work on your behalf for fees.

Public Record Office:
Tel: 081-876-3444

Chancery Lane
London WC2A 1LR
Opening hours: 9.30-5.00 Monday to Friday;
      Census rooms 9.30-5.00 Monday to Saturday

Ruskin Avenue
Kew
Richmond
Surrey TW9 4DU
Opening hours: 9.30-5.00 Monday to Friday

the RFC badge

Quartermaster-Sergeant

Sergeant

Flight Sergeant

Corporal

Air Mechanic 1st class

NCO rank badges of the RFC

the RFC pilot's badge

RNAS officer's cap badge c. 1915

the Observer's badge, 1915

Service badges of the First World War

SECTION ONE
British Military Flying until November 1918
by
Simon Fowler

Aviation in Britain before August 1914

Before the first heavier than air flights aeronautical interest centred on balloons. In particular, the military had long realised their potential for aerial reconnaissance. A Balloon Section of the Royal Engineers was established in 1879, and balloons accompanied several colonial expeditions in Africa during the 1880s and 1890s. A Balloon Factory was set up at Farnborough in 1897: the direct ancestor of the Royal Aircraft Establishment. Surviving records of the Balloon Section are in AIR 1. Of particular interest is AIR 1/723/69/1, which contains reminiscences of the Section in the 1880s and 1890s. A few early papers from the Balloon Section are in AIR 1/728.

Because they were impossible to steer, balloons had only limited use. During the 1880s and 1890s experiments were conducted in adding light motors to balloons. These motor driven airships were usually known as dirigibles. Leaders in the field were the Germans, Count Zeppelin being an early pioneer, and the French. Very little work was done in this field by the British until 1908. An interesting file on experimental airship flights between Crystal Palace and St Paul's Cathedral, London, in 1901 is in HO 45/10269/X86602.

British military authorities seemed equally uninterested in aircraft. Some correspondence about the purchase of a Wright Brothers' aircraft is in AIR 1/728/176/3/33, and the class also contains a few other items about the earliest flying machines. ADM 116/96 contains correspondence about the possible purchase of Cody kites for the Admiralty.

British military involvement in aviation stems from a report prepared by the Aviation Sub-Committee, under Lord Esher, of the Committee of Imperial Defence (CID) in 1909. This report is in CAB 4/3, and copies can be found elsewhere. It recommended that the Navy be allowed £35,000 to build an experimental airship and the Army £10,000 for experiments on navigable balloons. The report, however, saw 'no necessity for the Government to continue experiments in aeroplanes provided that advantage is taken of private enterprise in this form of aviation'.

The Balloon Factory, renamed the Army Aircraft Factory in 1911, became a centre for British research into aircraft design and construction. Because of the government's reluctance to support research by private companies the aircraft industry remained very small, in contrast to Germany, something which would have a serious effect during the first months of the First World War.

An Air Battalion was raised in 1911 as part of the Royal Engineers with the task of training men in handling balloons, airships and aircraft. Records of the Air Battalion are in AIR 1/1607-1609. AIR 1/1610 and 1624 also contain other material about British flying before the First World War.

A further sub-committee of the CID reviewed Britain's air preparedness and reported in February 1912. It recommended merging the small existing military and naval flying activities into a new Royal Flying Corps (RFC), which would have five sections: military and naval wings, a Reserve, a Central Flying School at Upavon, and the Army Aircraft Factory (renamed the Royal Aircraft Factory) responsible for aircraft design and production. A copy of the CID report which recommended setting up the RFC is in CAB 38/20. The RFC came into being on 13 May 1912. In July 1914 the naval wing broke away to become the Royal Naval Air Service (RNAS).

An Air Committee of the CID was established to co-ordinate the flying activities of both the Army and Navy. Its minutes and papers are in CAB 14, with other papers in AIR 1/2311 and 2317, and CAB 17.

There are a large number of files about the pre-August 1914 RFC in AIR 1. Readers interested in the subject should use the photocopied card index to the class, to be found in the Reference Room at Kew.

Considerable forethought had been given to planning the departure of the British Expeditionary Force to France in 1914. WO 106/51 contains the plan so far as it affected the move of aircraft and dirigibles to the continent.

Central direction of the air services in wartime

The development of the air services during the war was directed by events at the highest levels. In particular, politicians were concerned by service rivalry over aircraft production and the effectiveness of the air services, especially in defending Britain against air raids.

The Cabinet

At the outbreak of war in 1914 there was no Cabinet secretariat or even formal Cabinet minutes. The Prime Minister of the day summarized conclusions reached by Cabinet in letters to the Sovereign. This practice continued until the creation of the Cabinet secretariat in December 1916. Copies of the letters are in CAB 41 and occasionally refer to air matters. Papers discussed by Cabinet before 1916 are in CAB 37. These papers are listed in two PRO Handbooks: No 4 *List of Cabinet Papers, 1880 to 1914* and No 9 *List of Cabinet Papers 1915 and*

1916. Copies are available in the Reference Room.

In November 1914 the Cabinet appointed a War Council to consider general matters of war policy. The Council was latter superseded by the Dardanelles Committee (June to October 1915), and the War Council (November 1915 to November 1916). The Council took over many of the functions of the pre-war Committee of Imperial Defence. Minutes of the Committee and its successors are in CAB 22, with papers in CAB 42.

When Lloyd George became Prime Minister in December 1916 he established the Cabinet system as we know it today. For the first time formal minutes were taken of Cabinet meetings. In addition, Cabinet committees were set up as required. Both Cabinet itself and its committees were serviced by the Cabinet Office. The War Cabinet set up by Lloyd George comprised five (later seven) ministers, only one of whom had departmental duties. Chiefs of staff and other advisors regularly attended meetings. Minutes of the War Cabinet are in CAB 23, with papers in CAB 24. Subject indexes exist for both minutes and papers and are available in the reading rooms. Registered files on a variety of subjects, including a few on air matters, are in CAB 21. A collection of War Council and War Cabinet minutes and papers on air matters is in AIR 1/678/21/15/2102.

The development of the Cabinet system and its records is discussed more fully in PRO Handbook No 11: *The Records of the Cabinet Office to 1922.* Copies are available in the Reference Room.

The Supreme War Council was set up in November 1917 to direct the efforts of the various allied forces. Papers of the Council are in CAB 25, with minutes in CAB 28. Other papers of the Council relating to air matters are in AIR 1/2295-2300. The Council set up the Inter-Allied Aviation Committee whose papers are in AIR 1/27/15/1/179.

Central control of the air services

Until 1916 there was very little co-ordination between the two services. This was particularly acute with regard to the supply of aircraft, where both the War Office and the Admiralty had radically different systems of aircraft procurement which led to rivalry and conflict. For the public the weaknesses of the air services were demonstrated by their inability to shoot down Zeppelin raiders over Britain. This led to the decision of the War Council in February 1916 to hand over home aerial defence to the RFC.

A Committee on the Administration of the Royal Flying Corps was set up to investigate the efficiency of the RFC. Its minutes and papers are in AIR 1/516-519, with the final report in AIR 1/2317/223/20 and AIR 1/2405/303/4/5. The importance of the Committee, however, was soon overshadowed by other developments.

In February 1916 the War Council set up the Joint War Air Committee under Lord Derby. It was not a great success, because it had few powers and could not force agreement between the services. Papers of the committee are in AIR 1/2319.

The Committee was replaced by the Air Board, under Lord Curzon, which met between May and December 1916. It too was denied effective executive power. Reports of the Board are in CAB 42, and its Minutes in AIR 6, with some papers in AIR 1/2311.

The Air Board was given the task of co-ordinating air policy between the two services in January 1917, especially regarding aircraft procurement. For the first time it had executive powers. Lord Cowdrey was appointed as President of the Air Board. He was succeeded by Lord Rothermere in November 1917.

Responsibility for supply of aircraft passed to the Aircraft Production Department of the Ministry of Munitions in January 1917. Questions of policy, programme and design, however, remained with the Air Board. Records of the Department are in MUN 8, MUN 3/106-110, MUN 10 and AIR 1.

Continuing German air raids in the spring of 1917 prompted the War Cabinet to ask General Jan Smuts, a prominent South African soldier and statesman, to investigate the efficiency of the air services. His committee, the Committee on Air Organization and Home Defence against Air Raids, recommended that the RFC and RNAS be united. Reports produced by the Committee are to be found in CAB 21/21 and CAB 24. The War Cabinet approved Smuts's final report in August 1917.

In October 1917 the War Cabinet set up several committees under Smuts's chairmanship to organize the new Air Service and to plan long-distance raids against Germany. The most important of these committees was the Air Policy Committee. Minutes and papers of the committees are in CAB 27/9 and AIR 1/678/21/13/2102.

The Air Ministry and Royal Air Force (RAF) were established by the Air Force (Constitution) Act 1917. The Air Board, renamed the Air Council in January

1918, was given the task of setting up the RAF and the Air Ministry. The Air Council, however, lost responsibility for aircraft design and policy, which passed to the Aircraft Production Department of the Ministry of Munitions. Minutes of the Air Council are in AIR 6. A secretary of state for air was to answer for the Ministry in Parliament. The professional head of the RAF would be chief of the air staff.

The Royal Air Force was set up on 1 April 1918. It was the first independent air service in the world. Within a month of its formation both the secretary of state (Lord Rothermere) and the first Chief of Air Staff (Sir Hugh Trenchard) had resigned. There were also huge administrative problems in setting up the new Air Ministry in a relatively short time. Most of the work of the new RAF lay in supporting the British armies in France.

At the end of the war in November 1918 the need for a separate air service was much reduced. The RAF was rapidly slimmed down from 188 squadrons to just thirty-three. The post-war role of the RAF is discussed below.

A good introduction to the tangled administrative history of the establishment of the RAF is Malcolm Cooper, *The Birth of Independent Air Power* (1986).

The organization of the air services

The Royal Flying Corps (RFC)

From January 1914 the RFC (and later the RNAS) was organized in squadrons of three flights of four aircraft each plus three reserve aircraft, although this number tended to fluctuate greatly during the war. Until early 1916 squadrons had a number of roles in reconnaissance, artillery spotting, and bombing. After this date squadrons were usually assigned specific tasks. Squadron strengths were also increased to eighteen machines per squadron, and by the end of the war some fighter squadrons had twenty-four aircraft on their books at any one time.

The organization of the RFC altered dramatically during the war to meet both its rapid expansion and its changing role in the field. Upon the outbreak of war, the four squadrons of the RFC, totalling 105 officers, 63 aeroplanes and 95 units of motor transport, were sent to France, under the command of army headquarters. Left at home were 116 aircraft (described as 'mainly junk'), 41 officers and a few hundred airmen.

In November 1914 two Wings, of two squadrons each, were formed; 1st Wing to serve with the First Army, 2nd Wing with the Second Army. 3rd Wing was created in March 1915 and each then was enlarged to three squadrons. In August 1915 brigades, one for each Army, were set up, which comprised two wings of aircraft and a balloon wing. The brigade, commanded by a brigadier-general, was intended to supply the air needs for an army.

The RFC had twelve squadrons by October 1915 and twenty-seven by July 1916.

The Royal Naval Air Service (RNAS)

The RNAS was originally the Naval Wing of the RFC. The Admiralty took back control of the Wing from the War Office in July 1914 and it became known as the Royal Naval Air Service. Wags thought that RNAS stood for 'Really Not a Sailor'!

Until February 1916 it was responsible for the air defence of Britain (which was then transferred to the RFC), and was the pioneer of strategic bombing against Germany and sites in occupied Belgium from its base in Dunkirk. In addition, the RNAS continued its naval patrols from coastal air stations in Britain and from ships, including by 1918 the first aircraft carriers. The RNAS was organized in a similar way to the RFC, with squadrons and wings.

Many of the most important documents on the history of the RNAS appear in Capt S W Roskill, *Documents relating to the Naval Air Service, Volume I: 1908-1918* (Naval Records Society, 1969).

The Royal Air Force (RAF)

The split between RFC and RNAS led to bitterness, confusion and inefficiency (see the section on the central direction of the war above). So on 1 April 1918 the Royal Air Force was established, merging both the military and naval air services. At the time of the armistice it was 188 squadrons strong, with 22,647 aircraft and 103 airships on strength and 27,000 officers and 264,000 other ranks.

The organization of the RAF was based on that of the RFC and did not change much during the remaining few months of the war. One innovation, however, was the establishment of the Independent Air Force, under Sir Hugh Trenchard, to lead strategic bombing attacks on Germany.

RNAS squadrons absorbed into the RAF were given the new squadron number by adding 200 (ie 1 RNAS squadron became 201 Squadron RAF). Similar RNAS wings added 60 to existing numbers (ie 3 Naval Wing became 63 Wing RAF).

Central administration

Operationally the RFC, RAF and where appropriate RNAS units were under the control of the Army. Organizationally, however, control of the RFC rested with the Army Council, whose records are in WO 163. The Admiralty Board controlled the RNAS and its records are in ADM 167. For attempts to co-ordinate the efforts of both services see above.

Day to day orders about organization are to be found in the RFC HQ Routine Orders in AIR 1/805-809 (July 1913 - August 1914), 829-832 (August 1914 - December 1916), AIR 1/871-874 (January 1916 - June 1918) and AIR 1/835 (November 1917 - 1919). Brigades, Wings, Groups and Squadrons also issued routine orders and, where they survive, they are in this class. RAF Weekly Orders from April 1918 are in AIR 72.

The Women's Royal Air Force (WRAF)

As the War progressed women increasingly did the work of men, inside the armed forces as well as outside. Women were employed by the RFC, through the Women's Army Auxiliary Corps (WAAC), from early in 1917. The Women's Royal Naval Service (WRNS) was created in February 1918. Women mostly worked on air stations in Britain as clerks, cooks and in the workshops.

The Women's Royal Air Force (WRAF) was formed on 1 April from those women who were working for the RFC and RNAS on that date. By the armistice the WRAF numbered 25,500. After the war's end the WRAF was disbanded, and the last women left the service by November 1919.

Personnel records are held by the Ministry of Defence. There are virtually no records of the WRAF or its predecessors in the the PRO. A history of the WRAF prepared by the Air Historical Branch (AHB) in the early 1930s is in AIR 1/681/21/13/2212. A file on the work of the WRNS and later the WRAF in 5 Group is in AIR 1/106/15/9/284.

Operational records

When war broke out in 1914 it was believed that aircraft and airships would be most useful in locating enemy formations. New roles for the air services, however, were found as strategic needs changed and aviation technology advanced. By the end of the war aircraft were also engaged in strategic bombing, artillery spotting (that is, helping the guns find their targets), photographic reconnaissance, and, of course, in attacking enemy aircraft and airships.

Communiqués and summaries of activities

Summaries of activities were published by headquarters in weekly RFC and RAF Official Communiqués. The RNAS had a similar series of Operations Reports. The communiqués describe individual missions, including the shooting down of enemy aircraft and bombing raids and the names of pilots and squadrons involved.

Copies of RAF Communiqués are in AIR 1/2097/207/14/1. RNAS Communiqués between November 1915 and August 1918 are in AIR 1/2314/223/112. The RFC Communiqués for 1915 and 1916 have been published in Christopher Cole (ed), *Royal Flying Corps Communiqués 1915-1916* (1969) and the RAF Communiqués for April to November 1918 in Christopher Cole (ed), *Royal Air Force Communiqués 1918* (1969).

The RAF Museum has a complete set of RAF communiqués, and a largely complete set of RFC communiqués and a number of RNAS Operations Reports.

The PRO does not appear to have any RFC Communiqués, although daily summaries of work undertaken by the RFC between July 1917 and February 1918 are in AIR 1/838. There are also a number of summaries of activities undertaken by the air services scattered throughout AIR 1. Daily reports from RNAS (later RAF Naval) Stations from January 1915 to September 1918 are in AIR 1/189-232, 235-251, 310-333.

Squadron records

The most detailed records of operations are usually to be found in the records of the individual units. The vast majority of these records are in AIR 1. An index to squadrons, and other units, is at the front of the class list. The value of these records varies considerably between squadrons. They may include record books, correspondence, routine orders, daily summaries and reports.

Many histories of squadrons were compiled by the AHB after the war and are in AIR 1/687-696, with others in AIR 1/163-184, 361-362. It is also worth looking at the records of the wing or brigade to which individual squadrons or other units were attached. Operations Record Books for the period of the Second World War, in AIR 24-AIR 29, often include a brief history of the activity of their predecessors during the First World War.

Many squadrons and other units produced magazines which give some idea of contemporary life. Many of these magazines are now kept by the RAF Museum.

The easiest places to trace the location of a unit or its place in the wider RFC or RAF are the Orders of Battle which are in AIR 1/2129/207/83/1. Weekly lists of the location of RFC, RNAS and RAF units, together with commanding officers between February 1917 and September 1918, are in AIR 1/2112/207/52.

Combat reports and logbooks

Combat reports filed by individual pilots are in AIR 1/1216-1228. Many other combat reports are to be found elsewhere in AIR 1. You should treat these reports with some caution, as pilots tended to report multiple sightings of planes shot down. The British claimed 7,054 victories from June 1916 to the armistice. However, according to post-war calculations, the Germans only lost 3,000 aircraft.

Samples of airship logbooks are in AIR 3. A few pilot's logbooks from the First World War are in AIR 1 and AIR 4. Many logbooks, however, are kept by the RAF Museum.

Aerial reconnaissance

Much time and effort was spent in taking and analysing photographs of enemy positions. In the first years of the war photographs were normally taken from tethered balloons near the front line. But as cameras and machines developed this work increasingly came to be done by aircraft.

An introduction to the developments in aerial photography during the war is in AIR 41/6. A modern useful introduction to the subject is in the *NAPLIB Directory of Aerial Photographic Collections in the United Kingdom* (1993).

Papers on the technical development of aerial photography are in AIR 1/888-902. Some aerial photographs are in AIR 1/2269-2279.

A collection of photographs of defence works on the Western Front taken in 1916 and 1918 is in AIR 34/735. Two albums of photographs taken in 1917 are in AIR 10/200-201. AIR 10 (code 5) also includes some manuals of photography, including a number of interpretation guides to photographs such as AIR 10/1120. A small collections of photographs from the Western Front is in WO

316 and of the Battle of Messines in WO 158/306. Collections of photographs are held by the Imperial War Museum, but they can be difficult to use.

General reconnaissance reports from 1914 and 1915 are in AIR 1/2135-2140. They do not contain any photographs, however.

Bombing

Bombing of enemy targets developed very quickly on the outbreak of war. After only six weeks of the war the RNAS bombed Zeppelin sheds at Dusseldorf in Germany (see AIR 1/2099/207/20/1). In comparison with the Second World War strategic bombing never really developed to its full potential. This was largely because of uncertainty amongst war leaders as to its effectiveness.

Bombing was pioneered by the RNAS. Reports on operations between July 1916 and October 1917 are in AIR 1/62-63. Many operations were initiated by the Naval Air Station at Dunkirk. Bombing reports from the Station for the period April 1916 to March 1918 are in AIR 1/320-333. No 3 Naval Wing attacked many towns in South Western Germany between October 1916 and April 1917. Its operations were curtailed in April 1917 in order to divert resources to the RFC. Records of this Wing are in AIR 1/111-115.

41st Wing was set up by the RFC in late 1917 to attack German towns and cities. It was intended in part as retaliation for German air attacks on Britain. Records are in AIR 1/1749-1752, 2198.

During the winter of 1917/18 the War Cabinet agreed to a policy of strategic bombing and established the Independent Air Force (IAF), sometimes known as the Independent Force. The IAF evolved out of the 8th Brigade, RFC. It was still expanding at the time of the armistice, so never reached full effectiveness. Records of the 8th Brigade are in AIR 1/1649-1657 and the IAF in AIR 1/1972-2000, although there are a number of other documents about the Force scattered through AIR 1. Reports of bombs dropped between January 1916 and December 1917 are in AIR 1/840-842. AIR 1/2691 is a summary of bombing missions in 1917 and 1918.

After the end of the war a commission visited Germany to see how effective bombing had been. They concluded that although damage had been light, bombing had been effective in weakening morale in areas bombed. Their report is in AIR 1/2104/207/36.

A good introduction to the subject is Neville Jones, *The Origins of Strategic Bomb-*

ing: A study of British Air Strategic Thought and Practice up to 1918 (1973).

Like their successors a generation later, RFC and RAF pilots spent many hours in dropping propaganda leaflets. Samples of these leaflets, between 1916 and 1918, are in WO 32/5140-5143.

Anti-submarine attacks

One of the main duties of the RNAS was to locate and if possible destroy German U-boats. Records of these attacks during 1917 and 1918 are in AIR 1/2314.

Air attacks on Great Britain

German air raids on the British Isles, although small in comparison with those between 1940 and 1945, caused great panic and crisis at the highest levels of government, which directly led to the creation of the RAF. Britain's air defence rested with the RNAS until February 1916; thereafter responsibility passed to the RFC and later the RAF.

The first German raid on Britain took place in January 1915 and the last in August 1918. Raids took place infrequently and by small numbers of Zeppelin airships or, towards the end of the war, aircraft. They caused relatively little damage.

There are several series of intelligence reports on the raids in AIR 1/2123-2124, 2319-2320, and WO 158/935-960. Other reports and summaries can be found in the records of squadrons and other units in AIR 1. Other reports on the raids are in AIR 1/2420/305/8. Photographs of damage done by German air raids in 1915 and 1916 are in AIR 1/943/204/5/984.

The raids, however, caused some dislocation in industry and the railways. There are a few unimportant records in HO 45 (in the cut 'war'). Files on air raid precautions taken by the war industries are in MUN 4. A number of railway records relate to air raids. They are described in the index cards to the RAIL classes in the Reference Room at Kew (indexed under Air, Great War, War).

Operations other than on the Western Front

The air services operated in almost all theatres of war. The most important records are described below. You should remember, however, that much more on individual operations can be found in the records of individual units in AIR 1.

Dardanelles

A small number of RNAS aircraft helped with aerial reconnaissance during the abortive landings on Gallipoli during 1915 and 1916. A report prepared by the AHB after the war on the air operation is in AIR 1/681/21/13/3809. A roll of honour for RNAS officers is in AIR 1/675/21/13/1563. A number of aerial photographs of Gallipoli are in WO 317.

East Africa

A few planes were used in the campaigns in German East Africa (later Tanganyika, Tanzania) to look for German forces, in particular the German cruiser Koenigsberg. There are very few records of these operations in AIR 1. A summary of operations for April and May 1917 is in AIR 1/36/15/1/247. A narrative of the RNAS role in East Africa is in CAB 45/218.

Italy

Italy entered the war on the Allied side in 1915. Following Italian defeats at Caporetto in later 1917 the 14th Wing RFC (later RAF) was sent to northern Italy. A summary of operations by the Wing is in AIR 1/2128. A few other records are scattered through AIR 1. Some aerial reconnaissance photographs are in WO 323.

Mesopotamia

A small air unit was attached to the Expeditionary Force which landed in what is now Iraq early in 1915 to attack Turkish forces there. It initially engaged in photo reconnaissance activities. Towards the end of the war, however, air power was used to control rebellious local tribesmen. This continued after the war.

A summary prepared by the AHB in the 1920s of the air role in the Mesopotamian Campaign is in AIR 1/674/21/6/87. Records of operations, including records from individual squadrons, during and after the war are in AIR 20/500-515, 552-563, 695-700, and 718-719. Other records, including war diaries, are in AIR 1/426-432, 2102, and 2203-2209. Aerial photographs of Mesopotamia taken during 1918 and 1919 are in AIR 1/2304/226/18/2.

Palestine

Apart from an abortive attack by the Turks on the Suez Canal in February 1915, the war in Palestine began in earnest in 1917. RFC and RNAS units were posted to Egypt to help protect the Canal and later to undertake reconnaissance work.

War diaries of the HQ RFC Middle East from November 1916 to March 1920 are in AIR 1/2361-2372. Those of the Palestine Brigade, RFC between October 1917 and November 1919 are in AIR 1/2210-2211. Other records of the Brigade are in AIR 1/1725-1730, 2328-2331. Aerial photographs of Palestine taken during 1918 and 1919 are in AIR 1/2304/226/18/2. Other photographs are in AIR 20 and WO 319.

Russia

The Allied intervention in Russia strictly falls outside the period of the First World

War. British forces landed at Murmansk in June and August 1918 ostensibly to protect Allied war munitions, although their real aim was to help White Russian forces fighting the Bolsheviks. British troops also entered Southern Russia through the Caucasus at the same time. These forces included components from the RAF.

Papers of the RAF HQ in Southern Russia between 1918 and 1920 are in AIR 1/1956-1963. Communiqués issued by the command are in AIR 1/2130. Reports on operations in the Caspian Sea are in AIR 1/8/15/1/18 for February to August 1919. Records in AIR 20, described above in the section on Mesopotamia, also relate to operations in Turkey, Persia and the Caucasus during 1918 and 1919.

Monthly reports of operations in Northern Russia in 1918 and 1919 are in AIR 1/435/15/274/2-3. Reports and logs of the Dwina River Force are in AIR 1/438. Detailed records of the Syren Force are in AIR 1/1768-1770. They include operation records, logbooks and nominal rolls.

Aircraft and airships

Experimental establishments

The Army Aircraft Factory was formed in 1911 from the Balloon Factory. It was renamed the Royal Aircraft Factory, a year later, and became the Royal Aircraft Establishment in April 1918 to avoid a confusion of initials with the RAF.

In its early years the Factory combined research into aircraft design with aircraft construction. Plans of aircraft, engines and other equipment built at Farnborough between 1911 and 1918 are in AVIA 14. Logbooks recording all flights made from Farnborough with details of aircraft flown, names of pilots and duration of flights are in AVIA 1. They begin in 1914. Diaries of day to day activities of the Royal Aircraft Factory from 1911 to 1912 are in AIR 1/2404.

Technical reports, from 1916, are in AVIA 6. Some early reports and other correspondence are in AIR 1/729-732. The Admiralty equivalent to Farnborough was on the Isle of Grain. Reports of tests on aircraft in 1913 and 1914 are in AIR 2/164. Other reports are in AIR 1/1201-1206. Results were often published in the series of Admiralty Air Department Pamphlets to be found in AIR 1/2103. The Air Board set up the Aeroplane and Armament Experimental Establishment at Martlesham Heath in 1917. Early reports from the Establishment are in AIR 1/1190-1197.

The Advisory Committee (later Council) for Aeronautics was set up in 1910. It comprised a number of scientists and engineers who advised on the design of aircraft. Reports prepared by the Committee are in DSIR 23, with minutes and papers of the main and various sub-committees in DSIR 22.

AIR 1/697-717 include technical notes for aircraft produced by the Technical Branch of the Air Ministry and a number of air diagrams of aircraft. Similar notes produced by the Aircraft Production Department of the Ministry of Munitions are in MUN 8 and MUN 10.

Aircraft

The Public Record Office holds no sets of records for individual aircraft. Nor does the Office hold records of aircraft makers. A database to individual aircraft compiled from records in AIR 1 is being compiled. When it has been completed a copy will be placed in the Reference Room, but this is unlikely to be before 1996. The National Register of Archives, Quality House, Quality Court, London WC2A 1HP may be able to advise where existing records of individual companies are kept, although relatively few records for this period still survive.

The PRO, however, does have a great deal to interest the student of aircraft development, especially in the records of the Royal Aircraft Factory at Farnborough and the other research establishments. For example, plans of aircraft built at Farnborough between 1911 and 1918 are in AVIA 14.

Provided that the unit is known it may be possible to trace individual aircraft through squadron and other unit records in AIR 1.

A record of numbers assigned to service aircraft between 1915 and 1931 is in AIR 20/761. Lists of aircraft sent to France between April and June 1917 are in AIR 1/886-887.

Reports of aircraft (and pilot) casualties on the Western Front between March 1916 and April 1919 are in AIR 1/843-860, 865. Casualty cards held by the RAF Museum also give details of aircraft. For further information see above.

A few courts of inquiry into crashes in 1913 and 1914 are in AIR 1/777-778, 795-796. AIR 1 also contains a number of personal reminiscences about flying early aircraft. Some photographs are in AIR 1/728/176/3/38 and AIR 1/729/ 176/5.27-58. Reports on early aircraft are often to be found in the pages of *Flight* and *The Aeroplane* magazines. Copies of these magazines are with the RAF Museum.

Reports on the types of aircraft used in 1917 and 1918 are in AIR 1/1066-1070, 1075-1077, 1091-1093, 1109-1110. Reports on aircraft performance, with photographs, dating from 1919 are in AIR 1/454/15/312/9.

Air Publications are official publications mainly to do with the construction, maintenance and operation of aircraft and equipment. The main series of Air Publications begin in 1918 and are found in AIR 10, although the class contains some earlier examples. Air Publications, for the period between 1916 and 1918, are in AIR 1/2426-2428.

Other papers about aircraft can be found in AIR 2 (code 5/1) and AIR 5 (code 5/1).

Many Air Publications, and other aircraft manuals, are held by the RAF Museum.

Before January 1917 the procurement of aircraft was the responsibility of the two service ministries. After this date this work was taken over by the Ministry of Munitions. Some files are in AIR 1. Other pieces are in MUN 5/211-214 and MUN 8.

Equipment

Much about the construction, maintenance, and testing of equipment used in aircraft and elsewhere by the air services can be found in the records described in the aircraft and experimental establishments sections above. One notable exception is the collection of selected machine engine logbooks dating between 1913 and 1917 in AIR 1/2055-2076. Other tests on engines are in AIR 1/1094-1108. A few records of the RFC Directorate of Aircraft Equipment are in AIR 1/2429.

Reports of the Admiralty's Experimental Armament Department between 1916 and 1918 are in AIR 20/488-499.

Plans of engines and other equipment built at Farnborough between 1911 and 1918 are in AVIA 14.

Airships

In the early years of the century it was thought that airships, or dirigibles, would be more capable of military use than the aircraft. Germany especially concentrated on airship design and she had a considerable lead when war broke out. Britain too had a modest research and building programme which is reflected in the papers of the Balloon Factory from 1900 to 1911 in AIR 1/728-729.

Papers about pre-war airships are in AIR 1/1610-1624. A register of British airships built between 1911 and 1919, their career and eventual fate is in AIR 1/2315/222/6/A. Logbooks of some individual airships are in AIR 3. One or two may also be in AIR 1.

The Royal Airship Works was established by the Admiralty at Cardington near Bedford in 1917. It was responsible for designing and building airships. Papers of the Works are in AIR 11. Airship and engine drawings are in AIR 12. Other drawings of airships are in AVIA 24. Photographs of some airship sheds and seaplane bases are in AIR 59.

Other papers about the development and operation of airships are in AIR 2 (code 6/1) and AIR 5 (code/1).

Tethered balloons stationed behind the trenches played an important role in observing the success of artillery barrages and enemy activity in general. These balloons were the responsibility of the RFC (later the RAF) and records of Balloon Companies, Sections and Wings are in AIR 1.

Aerodromes and airfields

The air services overseas had few permanent bases. Squadrons tended to operate from makeshift airfields, as aircraft of the period normally only needed grass fields to land on and take off from. It is thus very difficult to find about individual airfields outside the British Isles, especially as, unlike those in the Second World War, airfields did not keep a daily record of events. There is very little in AIR 1, although it might be possible to find some information from squadron records. There is, however, a much greater likelihood of finding material for the larger permanent airfields such as the RNAS Air Station at Dunkirk. Individual air stations are listed in the index at the beginning of the class list.

In 1918 a survey of RAF stations in the British Isles was carried out and a directory issued in six volumes. These directories are in AIR 1/452-453.

A collection of photographs of RFC and RNAS aerodromes behind the Western Front, taken during June and July 1917, is in AIR 1/1078/204/5/1679. Other photographs of aeroplane hangars and seaplane bases taken by the RNAS Directorate of Works are in AIR 59. These photographs also include airship sheds.

Using the photocopied card indexes to AIR 1 in the Reference Room, it may be possible to find references to individual airfields or stations in the class. Records about individual airfields in Britain are occasionally also to be found in AIR 2 and AIR 5. Some drawings of buildings and a few site plans of airfields in Britain are held by the RAF Museum.

Foreign aviation

As might be expected the air services took a great interest in foreign, especially German, aviation. History sheets for German airships are in AIR 1/549/16/15/22. Crew lists of members of the German airship services in 1918 are in AIR 1/549. Notes and photographs of German airships for the war period are in AIR 1/6A. Interrogation of German prisoners of war, captured when their airships were shot down, are in AIR 1/541.

There are a number of reports of tests of captured German aircraft, for example in AIR 1/1 and 1036-1038. Lists of known German airmen serving in 1918 are in AIR 1/1975/204/273/27.

There is rather less for the aviation services of other countries. British air services used many types of French aircraft during the war and papers about these aeroplanes may be found in the records described above. There are a few papers on the French air services in AIR 1/2114-2115. Résumés of French operations are in AIR 1/881.

Reports on the progress of aviation in Italy between 1906 and 1914 are in AIR 1/2133.

Occasional reports about aviation abroad can be found in the Foreign Office General Correspondence in FO 371. A card index to the class is in the Reference Room.

Records of individuals

The overwhelming number of records about individuals in the air services during the First World War relate to pilots and to a lesser extent their observers. Pilots and observers were regarded as being the most important people in a squadron because they did the flying, the fighting and, in many cases, the dying.

You should remember that most men in the air services are not flyers. It has been estimated that during the First World War itself pilots and their observers made up rather less than one in twenty of the strength of the RFC. The rest were mechanics, riggers and other men (and occasionally women) who were responsible for maintaining the fragile aircraft.

A useful summary of the personnel records available before 1918 is *Personnel records (pre-1918)* (RAF Museum Information Sheet No 1, 1991) available free of charge from the Museum.

Service records

Records of service for members of the RFC and RNAS who continued to serve after 1 April 1918 are held by the RAF Personnel and Training Command, RAF Innsworth, Gloucester GL3 1EZ: Branch PG 5a(2) handles officers' records, whilst airmen's records are the responsibility of P Man 2b(1). Where men were killed or invalided from the service before this date their records are held by the Ministry of Defence, CS(R)2, Bourne Avenue, Hayes, Middlesex UB3 1RF. In all cases information is normally released only to the next of kin. You must also enclose a non-returnable fee (currently 15) with your enquiry. Service records are due to be transferred to the PRO during 1996.

Before the war

In the early years of the RFC would-be pilots were required to undertake training at civilian schools. Those who qualified for the Royal Aero Club's Aviator's certificates would have their fees refunded and could then be accepted for the Corps; they received training in military aviation skills at the Central Flying School at Upavon. The Royal Aero Club records, held by the RAF Museum, include a card index of holders of certificates. They give the pilot's date of birth, address, profession, and where and when he qualified for the certificate. Pilots were obliged to submit a portrait photograph with their application and most of these also survive. Once the services started setting up their own initial training schools fewer new pilots bothered to apply for a certificate.

Pre-war flights are described in the pages of *Flight*. There is a name index (officers only) to the magazine. Some wartime flights, mainly civil, are also described. In addition, the magazine includes regular lists of men who had gained the Royal Aero Club certificate. Copies of the magazine are held by the RAF Museum.

There is much less material at the PRO on pre-First World War flying. All officers in the RFC, including the Naval Wing, are listed in the monthly *Army List*. The *List* is in the Reference Room. A roll of pre-1914 RFC officers and NCOs has been printed in L McInnes and J V Webb, *A Contemptible little Flying Corps* (London Stamp Exchange, London, 1991).

AIR 1 contains some material about men in the RFC before August 1914. A roll of officers who joined the RFC in 1912 and 1913 is in AIR 1/803/204/4/1158, with service records for July and November 1912 in AIR 1/800/204/4/1084-1085. A list of NCOs holding flying certificates is in AIR 1/800/204/4/1073. When the RFC was set up in 1912 a large number of men applied to join the Reserve. Copies of letters sent to unsuccessful candidates are in AIR 1/362/15/231/1-2, AIR 1/363/15/231/3. AIR 1 also contains a number of reminiscences about the early days of flying.

First World War: introduction

There are many records which can shed light on a man's career in the air services, other than those described below. You should also remember that many men transferred to the RFC from other regiments or units.

These records are briefly described in Simon Fowler, *Army Records for Family Historians* (PRO Readers' Guide No 2, 1992). For a rather more detailed summary of the records available see Norman Holding, *World War 1 Army Ancestry* (Federation of Family History Societies, 1991), *More Sources of World War 1 Army Ancestry* (FFHS, 1991), and *Army records: a national directory of World War 1 sources* (FFHS, 1991). There is no equivalent for the Royal Navy or the RNAS.

Musters and lists

RFC officers are listed in the *Army List*. Officers in the RNAS are included in the *Navy List* (and are also briefly described in the *Army List*). A set of each *List* is to be found in the Reference Room. From the formation of the RAF on 1 April 1918 officers are given in the Air Force List. The only copy that the PRO has for the period of the First World War is for April 1918.

On the formation of the RAF a muster roll was compiled, giving brief information on NCOs and airmen. Copies are in AIR 1/819/204/4/1316 and AIR 10/232-237. The entries are arranged by service number. You must have a man's number before being able to trace his entry. There is no index to names.

There are a large variety of nominal rolls and other lists of personnel in AIR 1.

Of particular interest are AIR 1/761/204/4/153 - a list of pilots serving in August 1914, and AIR 1/765/204/4/237 - a list of all RFC men proceeding to France between August and November 1914. Nominal rolls of men in the RFC in January 1918 are in AIR 1/1214/204/5/2630. AIR 1 also includes a number of nominal rolls and lists for individual squadrons and other units. A list of British pilots who brought down ten enemy aircraft or more is in AIR 1/162/15/124/5. Miscellaneous lists of officers are scattered through AIR 1/827, 1283-1309. The location, or disposition, of RNAS officers between January 1916 and September 1918 is in AIR 1/2108-2111.

Officers attending the RAF Staff College during the early 1920s were asked to write up their wartime flying experiences. These very interesting accounts are in AIR 1/2386-2392. A nominal roll of airmen at Upavon in September 1914 is in AIR 1/793/204/4/804. Nominal rolls for other training schools between December 1914 and April 1916, together with copies of Royal Aero Club Aviation certificates, are in AIR 1/2432/306/1.

There are several books listing men of the air services, mainly pilots and observers. They include L McInnes and J V Webb, *A Contemptible little Flying Corps* (1991) which lists all NCOs in the RFC at the outbreak of war, together with short biographical details and photographs. Christopher Shores, Norman Franks and Russell Guest, *Above the Trenches: a complete record of the Fighter Aces and Units of the British Empire Air Forces, 1915-1920* (1990) contains biographical details for all aces, that is, pilots who shot down five or more enemy aircraft in combat. The PRO does not have copies of either book.

Casualties

The life of a pilot in the air services during the war was likely to be short but merry. Added to the dangers of combat was the ever present threat of aircraft or engine failure. Indexes to deaths of men in the air services are held at St Catherine's House, although they give very little information beyond name and date of death. French and Belgian death certificates for airmen who died in hospitals or elsewhere outside the immediate war zone are in RG 35/45-69. <u>These records are held at Chancery Lane.</u>

A roll of honour for members of the RFC and RNAS who died during the war is held by the Imperial War Museum, Lambeth Road, London SE1 6HZ. *The London Gazette* published weekly casualty lists and these were reproduced in the magazines *Flight* and *The Aeroplane*. Copies of *The London Gazette* are in ZJ 1.

Pilots and others who died between 1914 and 1917 are listed in Capt G C Campbell, *Royal Flying Corps: Casualties and Honours during the War 1914-1917* (1917). The PRO does not have a copy of this book, although copies are kept by the Imperial War Museum and the RAF Museum.

The most useful source for details of casualties are the sets of RFC and RNAS casualty cards held by the RAF Museum. These cards, however, are incomplete, especially for the earlier part of the war, and are mainly for casualties occurring in Britain or the Western Front. They give details about the reason for the casualty, type of machine and sometimes next of kin.

There are many lists and related correspondence about casualties in AIR 1/ 843-860, 914-916, and 960-969. Other useful sources are the various records of squadrons and other units in AIR 1. Some lists of RFC officers reported missing are in AIR 1/435/25/273/1-4.

You can obtain information on the location of graves of airmen from the Commonwealth War Graves Commission, 2 Marlow Road, Maidenhead, Berkshire SL6 7DX. The Commission may also be able to give information such as the date of death and unit.

Some hospital and medical records are to be found in the Army Medical Historian's papers in MH 106.

In a demonstration of chivalry for which the air war was famous, both sides regularly informed the other of pilots who had been captured, or indeed killed in action, by dropping messages over the other's airfields. Examples of messages dropped by German aircraft during 1916 and 1917, a number of which are very moving, are in AIR 1/435/15/273/11.

Honours and awards

Two sorts of awards were made to airmen; campaign medals and awards for bravery. Everybody who served in a particular campaign was entitled to a campaign medal. Copies of rolls of awards of the British War Medal, Victory Medal, 1914 Star, 1914-1915 Star, Territorial Force War Medal and Silver War Badge are in WO 329. They are for both officers and other ranks of the RFC and RAF. There is a card index on microfiche, in the Microfilm Reading Room at Kew, arranged by name. PRO Leaflet 101 *Service medal and award rolls: First World War* explains these records in more detail.

Equivalent medal rolls for the RNAS have yet to be transferred to the PRO, although it may be possible to glean a little information from medal rolls in ADM 171. In going through ADM 171 it may help to know that men serving in the RNAS were placed on the books of HMS *Pembroke* until 2 February 1915, when they were transferred to HMS *President*.

It can be more difficult to find awards for bravery. As well as a record of the award of the medal, a citation was also normally prepared describing how the medal was awarded. Details of awards of medals and accompanying citations were published in *The London Gazette*. The practice of publishing citations in the *Gazette* declined from mid-1916. It can be difficult to find individual awards in the *Gazette*, so it is important to know the approximate date of the award. You should also note that there was always a delay between the receipt of the medal and its notification in the *Gazette*. Copies of *The London Gazette* are in ZJ 1.

Many citations and other correspondence on the award of medals are in AIR 1/1030-1033, and in the papers of individual squadrons and other units in this class. A list of men who won the Victoria Cross (VC) is in AIR 1/519/16/9/1, with copies of the citations printed in *The London Gazette* in AIR 1/2318/223/55.

A number of NCOs were awarded the Military Medal. The roll for this medal will shortly be added to WO 326.

Prisoners of war (PoWs)

Many British airmen ended up as German PoWs. There is no central list of these men and it is very difficult to find very much about them. The list of British and Dominion prisoners of war held by the Germans and Turks in mid-1916 in AIR 1/892/204/5/696 consists almost exclusively of soldiers. Records of interrogation of escaped men are in AIR 1/501/15/223/1. It is understood that some records are held by the Imperial War Museum.

For further information about PoWs see *Army Records for Family Historians* (section 16.10) or PRO leaflet 72, *Prisoners of War: documents to 1919 in the Public Record Office*.

Courts martial

Court martial records are closed for 75 years. Thus no records for the RAF have yet been made available. Court martial records of RFC officers and men are in WO 92 (officers) and WO 87 (other ranks). For further information see *Army Records for Family Historians* (section 12).

Annex: How to use AIR 1

The vast majority of documents at the Public Record Office relating to the history of aviation in Britain to the end of the First World War are to be found in AIR 1. This class comprises for the most part documents collected by the Air Historical Branch (AHB) of the Air Ministry for the Official History of the Royal Flying Corps (RFC), Royal Naval Air Service (RNAS), and Royal Air Force (RAF) in the First World War, which resulted in Sir Walter Raleigh and H A Jones, *The War in the Air: Being the Story of the Part Played in the Great War by the Royal Air Force* (6 volumes, Oxford, 1922-1937).

AIR 1 includes records from many sources, not just from the air services themselves, but also from the Admiralty and War Office. As a result there is little in either Admiralty or War Office papers at the PRO about the development of flying. As well as departmental files AIR 1 includes a variety of other material including squadron records, personal papers, technical memoranda and reminiscences from former officers.

Unfortunately the class is poorly arranged and some of the piece descriptions are inaccurate. There is, however, a useful index to where material in the class came from at the beginning of the list. This index also lists individual units, such as squadrons, whose records are in the class.

There is a detailed card index to the class, a photocopy of which is available in the Reference Room at Kew. This index includes references to ephemeral material which was destroyed before the class was transferred to the PRO.

Ordering documents from AIR 1

Unlike almost all other classes of records in the PRO, you must give BOTH the piece number and the former AHB number when ordering items from this class. The AHB number is almost always given in the column next to the piece number, thus:

1   4/26/6   1916-1917   Captured German aircraft:
                                                        reports and tests

To see this document order AIR 1/1/4/26/6.

In this Guide the full reference is normally given. The full reference however is not given when two or more files relate to the same subject. Where this occurs you will need to check the class list to find the full reference.

Example 1: Rigid Airship No 9

In the years before the First World War considerable attention was paid to the development of the airship as well as the aircraft. The Germans, led by Count Friedrich von Zeppelin, were leaders in this. The first airship built by the Royal Navy was Rigid No 1 in 1909. During the First World War the airship, because of its vulnerability to attack, proved to be a big disappointment. After initial attempts to use them for observation purposes on the Western Front, most British airships spent the war in sea patrols tracking German U-Boats and raiders.

There are a number of documents about development of airships in AIR 1. Other records mainly for the inter-war period are in AIR 2. Probably the most important wartime record is the register of British airships built between 1911 and 1918 which describes where they were built, where they were based and their fate. This register may be found in AIR 1/2315/222/6/A.

The entry for Rigid No 9 indicates that it was built at Vickers yard at Barrow in Furness, and arrived at the RNAS Station at Howden, near Hull, on 4 April 1917. It spent most of its career at Howden, but also spent short periods at East Fortune, Cranwell and Pulham. By the time it was deleted from service, presumably broken up, on 28 June 1918 it had flown 4508 miles over 198 hours 16 minutes.

There are few other records about the airship in AIR 1. A photograph, however, is in AIR 1/728/176/3/38. Logbooks for some airships are in AIR 3, although one does not survive for Rigid No 9. Photographs of the airship sheds and other buildings at Howden are in AIR 59/5, although they do not identify individual airships. No records of Howden survive in AIR 1, although daily reports from RNAS Stations are in AIR 1/189-232, 235-251, and 310-333.

Example 2: The shooting down of the Red Baron: 21 April 1918

Count Manfred von Richthofen was the most famous German pilot of the First World War. His exploits as an ace in shooting down allied aircraft were celebrated in Germany and his fame spread rapidly to England and France. His dashing all red Fokker aeroplane and the Jagdstaffel or Circus he commanded were feared all along the Western Front. His end, however, came at about 10.45 am on 21 April 1918 when he was shot down by Captain A Roy Brown of 209 Squadron RAF, a Canadian from Toronto.

There are numerous records in AIR 1 about the dog-fight between Brown and von Richthofen. This is partly because some ten years after the incident the AHB compiled a memorandum based on an account in the *Chicago Tribune*, probably for inclusion in the Official History, which reflected a continuing interest in the Red Baron by the public.

The basic source for the study of any aerial combat for this period is the combat report. Combat reports were compiled either by the pilot or his observer after they landed. They should, however, be treated with some caution as pilots in the heat of battle often claimed aircraft which they had not shot down. There seems to be no doubt here that Captain Brown did shoot down the Red Baron.

His report is amongst other 209 Squadron combat reports in AIR 1/1228/204/5/2634, f 23. In it he notes: '[I] dived on a large formation of 15-20 Albatross scouts, D5s and Fokker triplanes, two of which got on my tail and I came out. Went back again and dived on a pure red triplane which was firing on Lt. May. I got along burst into him and he went down vertical and was observed to crash by Lts Mellersh and May. I fired on two more but did not get them.' A brief summary of his flight is noted in the Squadron Record Book (AIR 1/1858/204/214) which notes a 'decisive combat with Red Triplane' at 62B'.

Some ten years after the end of the war Captain Brown was interviewed about the shooting. Captain Brown's account (AIR 1/2397/262/2) is a vivid account not only of the battle with Richthofen, but also of the tremendous nervous strain that pilots were under. The report ends by noting that Captain Brown's nerves were still so bad that he was still unable to drive a car. Also in AIR 1 are copies of Richthofen's combat reports supplied by the German Military Historians in the late 1920s (AIR 1/2397/262/1).

Full records of 209 Squadron survive in AIR 1, from which you can flesh out an account of the Squadron's activities during the War. It is possible, for example, to discover the fate of Brown's Sopwith Camel. Papers in AIR 1/1857/204/214/5 show that it crashed on 5 May 1918 south of the Somme while being flown by Captain O W Redgate. At the time of the crash it had flown 51 hours 10 minutes. Other combat reports in AIR 1/1228/204/5/2634 give other impressions of the dog-fight. Lt May records: 'I fired at a second machine but without result. I then went down and was attacked by a Red Triplane which chased me over the lines low to the ground. While he was on my tail, Captain Brown attacked and shot it down. I observed it crash into the ground.' It is also possible to trace what happened to the pilots mentioned in the Combat Report. According to reports in AIR 1/1857/204/214/5 Captain Brown was admitted to 24 General Hospital on 24 May, presumably with his nerves. Lt Mellersh was retired to the Home Establishment on 3 May 1918 after fourteen months service. Lt May went on leave in July 1918, as the book notes a leave allowance being paid.

figure 1:   *Nulli Secundus* airship at Crystal Palace, 1907 (AIR 1/729/176/5/50)

The British Army airship *Nulli Secundus* was constructed in 1907 at the Army Balloon Factory at Farnborough. It was a semi-rigid airship with a length of 122 feet and a volume of 55,000 cubic feet, powered by a 50hp Antoinette engine. On October 5 1907, the airship flew from Aldershot to the Crystal Palace, to the fascination of the British public.

figure 2:   S F Cody in flight in the British Army Aeroplane No 1, 1909 (AIR 1/729/176/5/58)

On January 9 1909, the American aviator Samuel F Cody took off from Farnborough Common in his British Army Aeroplane No 1 for a short hop of 60 feet. The aircraft carried a Union Jack as well as ribbon streamers attached to the airframe, so that the effect of the airflow could be observed.

figure 3: Blériot monoplane (COPY 1/556, f 54249)

A photograph registered for copyright by Montague S F Dixon on 22 May 1911, showing Monsieur Pierre Prier in the cockpit of the Blériot monoplane in which he flew non-stop from Hendon to Issy, near Paris, on 12 April 1911. The panel was fitted with a roll-map and two instruments, while by his right knee was a pulsometer to indicate fuel. Prier was the chief instructor of the Blériot School at Hendon.

figure 4:   Parseval airship, 1915 (AIR 1/728/176/3/38)

Shortly before the First World War, Vickers acquired rights from the German
company of Parseval for the British Empire. The non-rigid Parseval naval
airship HMA No 6 made her first trials at Barrow in 1915 and was modified in
1918. The length was 312 feet, the volume 364,000 cubic feet, and the lift a
useful 7,052lb.

figure 5: Rigid Airship No 9 (AIR 1/728/176/3/38)

HM Airship No 9 was the first of Britain's rigid airships to fly, on 27 November 1916. After modification, she was accepted by the Royal Navy on 4 April 1917. Her length was 526 feet and she had a volume of 889,300 cubic feet. She was not a success, spending most of her time in mooring and handling experiments, and was dismantled in June 1918. This photograph clearly shows the huge size of the airship when compared to the spectators on the ground. The origin of the photograph is unknown, but it may have been taken during trials at Howden in 1917.

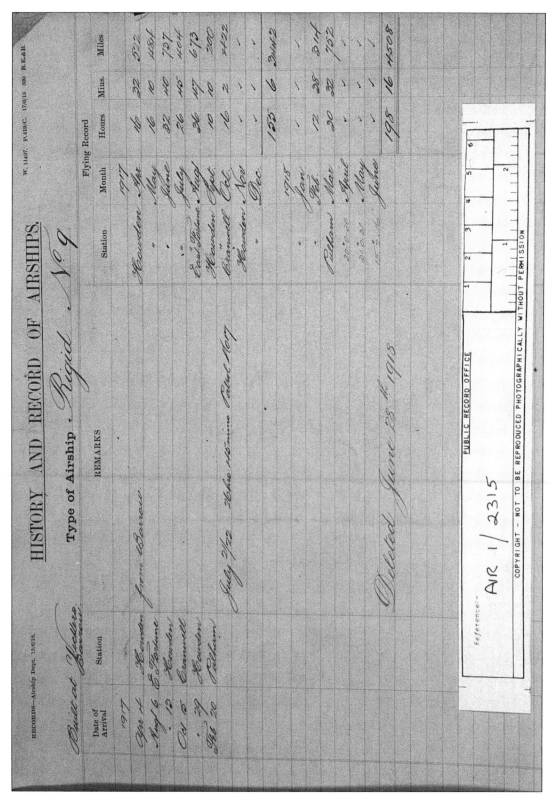

figure 6: The history and record of Rigid Airship No 9, 1917 (AIR 1/2315/222/6/A)

This volume briefly records the history of British airships from 1911 to 1918, describing where they were built, where they were stationed and their fate. Rigid No 9 was built at Vickers in Barrow in early 1917, spent much of its career at Howden and was deleted from the Service on 28 June 1918.

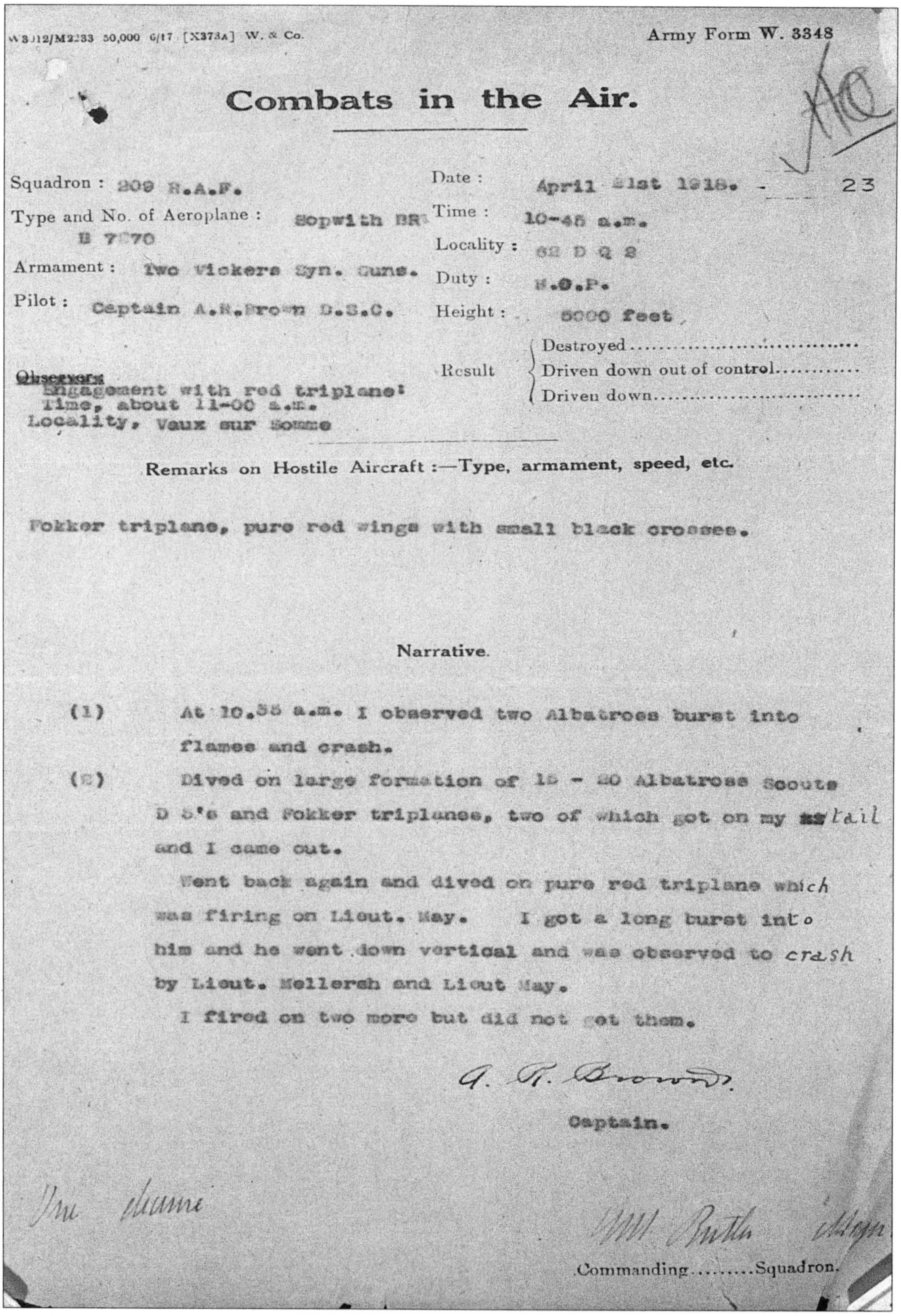

W.3.12/M2233 50,000 6/17 [X373A] W. & Co.　　　　　　　　Army Form W. 3348

Combats in the Air.

Squadron : 209 R.A.F.

Type and No. of Aeroplane : Sopwith BR
B 7270

Armament : Two Vickers Syn. Guns.

Pilot : Captain A.R.Brown D.S.C.

~~Observers~~
Engagement with red triplane:
Time, about 11-00 a.m.
Locality, Vaux sur Somme

Date : April 21st 1918.　23

Time : 10-45 a.m.

Locality : 62 D Q 2

Duty : H.O.P.

Height : 5000 feet

Result
Destroyed.........................
Driven down out of control...........
Driven down........................

Remarks on Hostile Aircraft :—Type, armament, speed, etc.

Fokker triplane, pure red wings with small black crosses.

Narrative.

(1)　At 10.55 a.m. I observed two Albatros burst into flames and crash.

(2)　Dived on large formation of 15 - 20 Albatros Scouts D 5's and Fokker triplanes, two of which got on my tail and I came out.

Went back again and dived on pure red triplane which was firing on Lieut. May. I got a long burst into him and he went down vertical and was observed to crash by Lieut. Mellersh and Lieut May.

I fired on two more but did not get them.

A. R. Brown.

Captain.

Commanding.........Squadron.

figure 7: Combat report by Capt A Roy Brown, 21 April 1918: shooting down of Richtofen (AIR 1/1228/204/5/2634, f 23)

Combat reports are essential for the study of dog-fights. The example here is the report for the shooting down of Count Manfred von Richtofen, the 'Red Baron'. It notes date, time and place, the reason for the operation and the aircraft used. Captain Brown was on an aerial observation mission in a Sopwith Camel.

figure 8: Sopwith Camel (AIR 1/728/176/3/38)

An aircraft similar to that flown by Captain Brown is shown in this photograph. A single engine biplane in service from the spring of 1917, the Sopwith Camel was the most used British fighter in the later years of the First World War and ultimately about 40 per cent of British fighters on the Western Front were Camels. A superb fighting machine, it was sufficiently versatile to be used as a light ground attack bomber, a night bomber, and in a maritime version flown from ships.

shoulder title

chief section leader rank badge

WRAF badges and insignia of 1918

Observer

Engineer

Air Bomber

Signaller

Medical collar badge

Flight Nursing Attendant   Flight Medical Officer

shoulder title   ward uniform badge

aircrew half-wing badges pre-1939   PMRAFNS badges of 1924

Inter-war service badges

SECTION TWO
The Inter-War Years
by
Peter Elliott

Historical background

The inter-war period saw the fledgling RAF struggling to establish itself in the face of cuts in defence spending and opposition from the Army and Royal Navy. During this period the foundations of the permanent RAF were laid and, through the vision of Lord Trenchard, institutions which would train its future officers and NCOs were created. Squadrons operating in the Middle East and India helped to keep the peace in those areas whilst, at home, the RAF kept itself in the public eye through record-breaking flights which pushed back the frontiers of aviation.

Personnel records

As individuals' records of service are held by the Ministry of Defence and are unlikely to be transferred to the PRO for some time, very few records are available which throw light on the careers of NCOs and airmen. With officers the situation is somewhat better. The *Air Force List*, which between the wars was published monthly, shows each officer's rank and seniority date. The index of names directs the reader to columns in which the officers are listed: these columns are grouped so that all the officers in a particular branch of the service (such as General Duties, Medical, Stores or Accounts) appear in order of rank and seniority. A set of the *Air Force List* is available in the lobby outside the Reference Room at Kew. In the 1920s and early 1930s the number of branches was small: most officers served in the General Duties Branch, and ground posts were filled by pilots who had undertaken extra training to enable them to serve a tour as, say, Engineering Officer to a Squadron.

Using the *List* published between April 1920 and April 1939 it is possible to trace an officer's postings. Much of the *List* is given over to details of RAF units (not only squadrons but also maintenance and training units): their locations and aircraft are shown, together with a list of the officers serving with each unit, including the date of their posting to the unit. The index of names generally directs the reader to two columns, one giving the officer's seniority and the other his posting. Officers serving in the Air Ministry are also detailed, together with senior civil servants. It is thus possible to trace officers' movements over many years relatively simply. Service numbers were not shown in the *Air Force List* until September 1939.

The Submission Papers in AIR 30 include material relating to awards and decorations - including changes to the rules governing the award of decorations - the appointment of senior officers and the granting of honorary commissions.

The Casualty Cards held by the RAF Museum include a few cards for men killed and injured during this period, including a fair number of sporting injuries! Although you can see the cards and either make or request transcripts, photocopies cannot be made. Some of the cards include summaries of the findings of Courts of Inquiry into accidents; most of the records of such courts have been destroyed but a few can be found in AIR 2, indexed under codes 1/1,1/3 and 22.

Medals

The RAF's operations in overseas theatres ensured that the Service's four awards for gallantry (the Distinguished Flying Cross [DFC], the Distinguished Flying Medal [DFM], the Air Force Cross [AFM] and the Air Force Medal [AFM]) continued to be awarded during the 1920s and 1930s, as was the DSO. From 1931 the Military Cross and Military Medal could be awarded to members of the RAF for gallant and distinguished service on the ground. Other awards such as the Empire Gallantry Medal and the British Empire Medal were instituted in 1922.

AIR 30 contains papers submitted to the Sovereign seeking his approval for the award of medals and honours: although these often relate to the New Year and King's Birthday honours lists, some citations are given. The main source for citations and for Mentions in Despatches is *The London Gazette* (ZJ 1), and recommendations for awards can be found in AIR 2, Code B 30. A list of recipients of the DFM has been published (I T Tavender, *The Distinguished Flying Medal: a record of courage 1918-1982*, Polstead, 1990) which gives the date of each award and, where appropriate, includes citations.

Few campaign medals were issued between the wars: those serving in India qualified for the India General Service Medal (IGSM), issued between 1908 and 1935; a new IGSM was instituted in 1938. Those serving in other theatres could qualify for the General Service Medal. With all these medals bars were worn showing the campaign in which the bearer had served, such as *North West Frontier, 1936-37*.

Regulations governing the award of these medals were issued in Air Ministry Orders (AIR 72). No medal rolls for campaign medals issued after the First World War are available, although a list of RAF holders of the 1908-1935 IGSM has been published (Anon, *India General Service Medal 1908-1935 to the Royal Air Force*). A copy is held in the RAF Museum library.

Women in the RAF

The Women's Royal Air Force, which had been formed in 1918, was disbanded in 1920. Most of the surviving records are in AIR 1. The RAF Nursing Service, which was set up as a temporary expedient in 1918, was formally established in 1921 and in 1923 became Princess Mary's Royal Air Force Nursing Service (PMRAFNS). Correspondence relating to the founding of the PMRAFNS can be found in AIR 2/93/C45714 and AIR 2/93/CW1528. The Service maintains a small archive, mainly consisting of photographs, which is in the care of the RAF Museum.

Training

Lord Trenchard set up three training establishments which were to play a crucial role in the life of the RAF.

The Royal Air Force College at Cranwell was opened in 1920 to train officers who would receive Permanent Commissions and form the backbone of the service. The course lasted two years and included pilot training. Many of the cadets who trained at Cranwell in the inter-war years went on to give distinguished service in the Second World War and later. The Old Cranwellian Association's *List of graduates 5 February 1920 - 30 April 1952* (Cranwell, 1952) lists every cadet entry and gives very brief details of each man. These details include the school he attended, the years of his cadetship, the rank he achieved as a cadet, College colours awarded for sport, the final RAF rank held, any decorations and, where appropriate, his fate. Copies of the list are held in the libraries of the RAF Museum and the RAF College. E B Haslam's book *The history of Royal Air Force Cranwell* (London, 1982) gives a good account of the formation and subsequent history of the College.

Not all officers were trained at Cranwell: it was realised that some men would not want a permanent career in the service but could serve for a number of years before moving on to the Reserve, to be called up in time of war. Those Direct Entrants selected for Short Service Commissions underwent officer training at the RAF Depot, Uxbridge and learned to fly at RAF Flying Training Schools. The term of service on the active list was set in 1919 at four years. In the 1930s a system of Medium Service Commissions was introduced.

The RAF Staff College was formed at Andover in 1922 and prepared experienced officers for service in headquarters and the Air Ministry. AIR 69 contains texts of lectures and students' papers, whilst the RAF Museum holds a number of folders containing synopses of lectures and exercises for most of the first 40 courses held between 1922 and 1950. Students on early courses wrote papers on their experiences in the First World War and subsequent conflicts: selected papers, many by officers who subsequently rose to very high rank, can be found as AIR 1/2385-2392. They were also issued as Air Publications, and therefore also appear as AIR 10/973, 1109, 1159, 1269 and 1703. The College's magazine, *The Hawk*, includes papers by students and also contains lists of course members. Copies are held by the RAF Museum, and also by the College which is now at Bracknell. However, the College now holds very little archival material.

Lord Trenchard also set up an apprentice scheme, to train boys for the most important trades. Many of these would become the RAF's future NCOs. The first Entry commenced training at Cranwell in January 1921, but later training for airframe and engine mechanics moved to Halton, near Aylesbury. The course lasted three years. Apprentice wireless mechanics and operators underwent a two-year course at the Electrical and Wireless School at Flowerdown, near Winchester. The School moved to Cranwell in 1929 and, after the Second World War, to Locking, near Weston-super-Mare. In 1934 the apprenticeship scheme was broadened to include Clerks, who were trained at the RAF Record Office at Ruislip, and in 1935 a Boy Entrant scheme was introduced as part of the RAF's expansion. Boy entrants underwent two years' training for selected trades such as Armourer. Adult entrants underwent their initial military training at the RAF Depot before learning their trade at trade training schools.

Pilots were trained either as part of the Cranwell course or at one of the RAF's Flying Training Schools; the latter were based in the United Kingdom and also in Egypt. From 1935 elementary flying training for officers on Short Service Commissions was carried out at civilian-run schools, and advanced training at Service Flying Training Schools. A history of RAF flying training can be found in AIR 32/14; a similar volume describing Reserve and Auxiliary flying training is in AIR 32/15. In each case the main body of the volume deals with training between the mid-1930s and 1945, but some information on earlier periods is included. Records of ground and flying training units can be found in AIR 28 and AIR 29.

Research and Development

During the 1920s and 1930s the RAF was at the forefront of technical development in aviation. The Royal Aircraft Establishment (RAE) at Farnborough was largely concerned with 'pure' research into aerodynamics, engines and so on, whilst the effectiveness of weapons and the performance of aircraft were evaluated by the Aeroplane and Armament Experimental Establishment at

Martlesham Heath. The files kept by the RAE are in AVIA 13, whilst the reports issued by the two establishments are to be found in AVIA 6 and AVIA 18 respectively. AVIA 1 contains the RAE's Flight Logs, which record virtually every test flight made at Farnborough over the period May 1914 to March 1954. These logs give only basic details such as the date, aircraft, pilot, duration and purpose: for example, with typically British understatement, Flight Lieutenant Swain's flight which set a new World Altitude Record on 28 September 1936 is recorded simply as 'H/A [High Altitude] Test'.

The Aeronautical Research Committee (renamed the Aeronautical Research Council in 1945) was originally founded in 1909. It advised the government on aeronautical research and supervised research being undertaken at the RAE and other establishments such as the National Physical Laboratory. Minutes of the Committee's meetings, together with those of its panels and sub-committees, are in DSIR 22, whilst reports and papers are in DSIR 23 and correspondence in DSIR 24.

The Marine Aircraft Experimental Establishment at Felixstowe carried out development work and trials on flying boats and marine craft: its reports are in AVIA 19. Trials involving the carriage and dropping of torpedoes and mines were undertaken by the Aircraft Torpedo Development Unit, formed in 1921 at Gosport; its files are in AVIA 32 and its reports in AVIA 16, although there are no Operations Record Books before 1941.

On the ground, two major developments were those of Radar, originally given the cover name Radio Direction Finding or RDF, and the jet engine. Sir Frank Whittle's papers on the development of the jet engine are in AIR 62 and component drawings are in AVIA 30. Material on the early development of radar is to be found in AVIA 17 (Air Defence Experimental Establishment reports) and AVIA 26 (Royal Radar Establishment reports and papers). The Air Ministry's Directorate of Research issued monthly reports between 1919 and 1925 on work in progress: copies are in AIR 60. Files relating to other inventions, covering the period 1915 to 1960, are in AVIA 8. Some correspondence on awards to inventors can be found in TS 28.

Air Publications are the RAF's series of technical manuals and training handbooks, and can be found in AIR 10. The contents of this class are classified into a number of subject groups, and there is also an index which converts AP numbers to piece numbers. The RAF Museum also holds an extensive collection of Air Publications.

Balloons and airships

Balloons and airships were the responsibility of the Royal Airship Works (later the Balloon Development Establishment) at Cardington. AIR 11 contains files on the design, construction and testing of airships, whilst drawings for a wide range of airships, including the ill-fated R101 and the R100, and their engines are in AIR 12. Files on the inspection of the R100 can be found in AIR 20/104-136 and 146-154, whilst a number of files relating to airships can be found in AIR 2 and AIR 5, in each case under codes 6 (particularly files concerning the inquiry into the loss of the R101) and 6/1. Logbooks for airships are in AIR 3.

Unit records

From the outset, King's Regulations required Commanding Officers to keep historical records of their units' activities. At first, squadrons continued to compile war diaries as they had done during the First World War but, by 1928, these had been replaced by the Operations Record Book (ORB). RAF Form 540 was to be used for the narrative account of a unit's work, whilst the appendixes, containing statistical and other data, were recorded on Form 541. A few inter-war unit records can be found in AIR 5, indexed under code 47/1, whilst ORBs compiled by units, ranging in size from Commands to Flights, and stations are in AIR 24 to AIR 29. The squadron ORBs in AIR 27 are available in the Microfilm Reading Room at Kew. A set of *Confidential Organizational Memoranda*, reporting the formation, movement and disbandment of units from 1933 to 1939, is held by the RAF Museum, whilst the 1939 volume of SD 155 *Secret Organizational Memoranda* is in AIR 10/1669.

Airfields and stations

At the end of the First World War the RAF undertook a survey of all its aerodromes in the United Kingdom. A directory - entitled *Quarterly survey of Royal Air Force Stations, British Isles* - was issued in six parts, and a set can be found in AIR 1. The volumes are as follows:

Volume I	Training stations
Volume II	Parks and depots
Volume III	Schools
Volume IV	Home defence stations and landing grounds (aeroplanes and balloons)
Volume V	Marine operations stations (seaplanes, aeroplanes and balloons)

> Volume VI   Airship, experimental and miscellaneous
>   stations

Volumes I and II have the reference AIR 1/452/15/312/26, whilst Volumes III to VI are in AIR 1/453/312/26. Another copy of Volume VI is in AIR 1/2118. It is not known whether the survey continued to be produced quarterly. A typical entry for a station records its location and function, the establishment (ie numbers of staff) and the accommodation provided, and includes a map of the site. In the case of airfields, brief meteorological information is given together with a description of the aerodrome.

The Air Ministry took over responsibility for the purchase and leasing of its land from the War Office in 1930. Although the RAF reduced considerably in size in the 1920s, there is much in the files in AIR 2 and AIR 5 relating to the purchase and leasing of land for aerodromes, training stations and bombing ranges. Appropriate references are to be found under the subject code 57/3.

The RAF Museum holds a large collection of Record Site Plans for RAF stations, together with drawings for a number of types of building. Although the majority of these date from the Second World War, there are many others from the First World War and the inter-war years. Another, smaller, set of Record Site Plans covering the period 1935 to 1945 is in AIR 20/7585-7586. Photographs of a number of airship sheds and aircraft hangars are in AIR 59, whilst WORK 44 contains representative drawings and plans of buildings such as the Officers' Mess at RAF Upavon and 'C' Type hangars. Station ORBs in AIR 28 summarize events in the life of the Station.

Operations

The service found its main work between the wars in helping to control warring factions in areas such as Iraq and Palestine. A crucial advantage of Air Control, or aerial policing, was the speed of response which air power provided, whilst a few aeroplanes could control a situation which would have required hundreds of troops. If trouble broke out, such as an attack on a Government fort, aircraft could be on the scene far quicker than troops who might have to travel hundreds of miles. Where a group of tribesmen were causing trouble, leaflets were dropped on their village warning that if they did not surrender, the village would be bombed. RAF Armoured Car Companies were formed in Iraq, Aden and Palestine to work with the aircraft. The ORBs compiled by squadrons operating in this role contain much useful information and can be found in AIR 27; the ORBs of the Armoured Car Companies are in AIR 29/50-56.

The speedy response offered by Air Control meant that fewer troops need be stationed in these areas, making it a more economical way of policing Britain's mandated territories and protectorates. Papers on the scheme can be found in AIR 8/45-46 and 122, AIR 9/12, AIR 20/526-551 and 566-586, and in AIR 19, whilst AIR 23 (Records of Overseas Commands) includes reports on specific operations. Other reports and summaries of operations in Palestine, Iraq, Aden, Somaliland and India can be found in AIR 5, under subject codes 40/4, 43, 45/7 and 56/1. A few reports were issued as Air Publications and can be found in AIR 10, indexed under code 1/1. Sir John Salmond made a tour of inspection in India in 1922 and his report is in AIR 8/46; other papers by him are held by the RAF Museum. There are unregistered papers relating to overseas operations in AIR 20/448-760. David E Omissi's book *Air power and colonial control* (Manchester, 1990) examines the concept of Air Control in depth.

Policy and planning between the wars

A good overview of policy in the 1920s and 1930s is given in H Montgomery Hyde's book *British aviation policy between the Wars* (London, 1976).

The Committee of Imperial Defence set the overall policy for the three services, and minutes of its meetings are in the CAB series of classes. Of particular interest are the papers of the Chiefs of Staff Committee (CAB 53), the Deputy Chiefs of Staff Committee (CAB 54), which includes papers of a Sub-Committee on Inter-service Training, and the Joint Planning Committee (CAB 55). All of these are available in the Microfilm Reading Room at Kew.

The Air Council discussed and formulated policy for the RAF and the Air Ministry; the minutes of its meetings and papers prepared for the Council are in AIR 6.

The RAF's *War Manual*, Air Publication 1300, was first issued in 1920 and sets out doctrine on a number of aspects of air warfare. It is one of many Air Publications in AIR 10 which were issued to disseminate policy and aid training: these are mainly indexed under code 1/1.

Although AIR 8 contains papers from the office of the Chief of the Air Staff, a large collection of Lord Trenchard's semi-official papers and correspondence is available on microfiche at the RAF Museum. The Museum also holds some of the papers of Sir Frederick Sykes, Chief of the Air Staff between April 1918 and March 1919.

From 1919 British military planning followed the assumption that there would be no major war within the next ten years. The so-called 'Ten Year Rule' was finally abandoned in 1933: by then it had become obvious that Britain had to prepare for war and a series of schemes was devised to expand the RAF. The Air Historical Branch (AHB) narrative on the expansion of the RAF is in AIR 41/8, whilst papers relating to expansion can be found in AIR 8 (Chief of the Air Staff) and AIR 9 (Director of Plans). Other relevant files are in AIR 20. AIR 19/1-11 comprise papers on the 'Shadow Factory' scheme by which British aircraft and aero-engine companies were able to increase production to cope with the expected demands of war.

As part of the RAF's expansion, the organizational structure of the service in the United Kingdom changed. In 1936 four Commands - Bomber, Fighter, Coastal and Training - were formed. This functional organization has continued, despite the formation of new Commands and their subsequent amalgamation. Annex 3 shows how the structure of the RAF has changed since 1918. Although the narratives in AIR 41 concentrate on the activities of the various Commands in the Second World War, many of them also describe inter-war developments. The ORBs compiled by the home Commands themselves are in AIR 24, and those of overseas Commands are in AIR 23. Files relating to plans made by Bomber, Coastal and Fighter Commands can be found in AIR 14-AIR 16.

The Air Ministry took over control of the Observer Corps from the War Office in January 1929. Control of the Corps was given to Air Defence of Great Britain, and in 1936 to Fighter Command; some papers relating to the Corps can be found amongst the Fighter Command files in AIR 16. Files on the Corps' involvement in the Air Exercises of 1930 and 1934 are in AIR 2, indexed under code 40/1.

For much of the inter-war period the Fleet Air Arm (FAA) was substantially manned by the RAF, but the Admiralty was unhappy with this arrangement and in 1937 it was agreed that control should pass to the Admiralty: Volume 1 of the AHB narrative *The RAF in maritime war* (AIR 41/45) describes the early years of the FAA and the arguments put forward by both sides. **Section Four** deals with FAA records in more detail.

Air Ministry Orders

Air Ministry Orders (AMOs) were a means by which information such as changes to regulations or temporary instructions could be disseminated. From 1931 the Orders were issued in a number of series: the A series were regarded as standing orders and dealt largely with administrative matters, whilst the N

series were ِ‌ ﹾunced the introduction (and withdrawal) of
equipment and‌ ﹾnd other matters. The E series dealt with
equipment. The ﹾ ﹾ in AIR 72; the RAF Museum holds virtually complete sets ﹾ ﹾs.

Records relating to ﹾ ﹾft

Although the Air Ministry k‌ ﹾnits to which each of its aeroplanes was allocated, most of tﹾ ﹾnt Cards (Air Ministry Form
78) for aircraft with serial numbe‌ late 'J' series have not survived. The cards which are extant a‌ Historical Branch (AHB)
of the Ministry of Defence; microfilm ﹾn at the RAF Museum,
and photocopies can be supplied. A h‌ ﹾtions used on these
cards is given in Annex 2 at the end of thﹾ

From as early as 1918 the Air Ministry compﹾ ﹾord cards (Air
Ministry Form 141, later AM Form 1180) which w‌ ﹾse the causes
of aircraft accidents. Few of the cards for accident‌ ﹾ-1930s survive; again, these cards are held by the AHB, with mﹾ Hendon.
Although you may use the microfilm and either makﹾ scripts,
photocopying is not permitted.

The aviation enthusiasts' society Air-Britain is publishing a ser‌ ﹾocu-
menting the histories of aircraft, using information from a vaﹾ ﹾr sources
including the cards described above, pilots' logbooks and unit records.

Annex 1: Other institutions holding relevant records

Royal Air Force Museum

The Museum was founded in 1964 and the Department of Research and Information Services holds extensive collections of documents, including the papers of a number of senior RAF officers, together with photographs, films, maps and technical manuals. Some of the collections are designated as public records, for example the Air Publications collection which contains far more than those held in AIR 10. There is also an extensive collection of aircrew flying logbooks covering all periods, theatres and aircrew categories.

The Department also has approximately a quarter of a million technical drawings, mainly manufacturers' drawings from companies such as Supermarine, Armstrong Whitworth and Bristol, together with Air Ministry plans for a number of RAF stations at home and abroad and buildings ranging from hangars to mortuaries. Documents relating to the history of the British aircraft industry include papers from the Handley Page, Fairey and Alvis companies.

The Reading Room is open to researchers by prior appointment, from Monday to Friday, 10 am to 5 pm.

Enquiries to: Department of Research and Information Services, Royal Air Force Museum, Grahame Park Way, Hendon, London NW9 5LL. Telephone 081-205-2266.

Imperial War Museum

The Museum was founded in 1917 and its research collections include documents, film, sound recordings, printed books and photographs, many of which are public records. The Department of Documents holds the papers of a number of high-ranking officers, together with captured German documents, whilst the Department of Printed Books has extensive collections of aerial propaganda leaflets, maps and technical drawings, including drawings produced by the Handley Page Aircraft Company.

At least 24 hours' notice should be given of an intended visit. The Reference Departments are open Monday to Friday, 10 am to 5 pm, and some offer a restricted service on Saturday.

Enquiries to the relevant Department (Art, Documents, Exhibits and Firearms, Film, Photographs, Printed Books, or Sound Records): Imperial War Museum,

Lambeth Road, London SE1 6HZ. Telephone 071-735-8922.

Liddell Hart Centre for Military Archives

Part of the Library of King's College London, the Centre holds papers presented by private individuals. These include letters, diaries, photographs and memoirs, and represent the work of statesmen, senior officers - including a number of Air rank - civil servants and others. The collection covers all aspects of military policy and operations in the twentieth century.

Enquiries to: Liddell Hart Centre for Military Archives, The Library, King's College London, Strand, London WC2R 2LS. Telephone 071-836-5454, ext 2187.

British Airways Archives

The archives comprise files, minute books and other records produced by British Airways and its antecedents - notably the British Overseas Airways Corporation (BOAC), British European Airways and Imperial Airways, but also including a number of smaller regional companies.

Enquiries and requests for access to the archives should be made to: British Airways Archives, Trident House, Block E S583, British Airways Plc, London Heathrow Airport, Hounslow, Middlesex TW6 2JA.

British Library Oriental and India Office Collections

The material formerly held by the India Office Library includes very little relating to the RAF in India. There are, however, a nominal index of RAF personnel serving in India between 1919 and 1939 and records relating to the pay of Indian personnel serving with the RAF in Britain in the 1940s and 1950s.

Enquiries to: British Library Oriental and India Office Collections, 197 Blackfriars Road, London SE1 8NG. Telephone 071-412-7873.

National Register of Archives

The NRA does not itself hold archives, but acts as an index to direct enquirers seeking the papers of individuals or companies to the repositories which hold them.

Enquiries to: Royal Commission on Historical Manuscripts, Quality House, Quality Court, Chancery Lane, London WC2A 1HP. Telephone 071-242-1198.

Defence Research Agency Aerospace Division

Formerly the Royal Aircraft Establishment (RAE). The Library holds an extensive stock of RAE reports (those held in the PRO are in AVIA 6) and a small amount of archive material relating to the history of the RAE.

Access is <u>strictly by appointment only</u> and applications should be made to: The Chief Librarian, DRA Aerospace Division, Farnborough, Hampshire GU14 6TD. Telephone 0252-304001.

Ministry of Defence Air Historical Branch

The Branch is responsible for writing official histories and answering requests, primarily from government departments and RAF units. Only limited assistance can be given to private individuals. Most of the material handled by the Branch is closed to the public, as it is less than thirty years old, but requests for assistance from bona fide researchers will be considered.

Enquiries to: Ministry of Defence, AHB(RAF), 3-5 Great Scotland Yard, London WC1A 2HW.

Annex 2: Abbreviations commonly found on Aircraft Movement Cards (AM Form 78)

AGS	Air Gunnery School
AGT	Airwork & General Trading (part of the CRO)
AST	Air Service Training (CRO)
Aw/Cn	Awaiting Collection
BATF	Beam Approach Training Flight
B&GS	Bombing & Gunnery School
CAT	Damage Category - see **Appendix 2**
(C)OTU	(Coastal) Operational Training Unit
CRO	Civilian Repair Organization
CRP	Contractor's Repair Party
CS(A)	Controller of Supply (Aircraft)
CWP	Contractor's Working Party
DBF	Destroyed By Fire
DBR	Damaged Beyond Repair
EANS	Empire Air Navigation School
E/F	Engine Failure
FA;F(A);F/A	Flying Accident - accidental damage or loss
FB;F(B);F/B	Flying Battle - operational damage or loss
FBSU	Flying Boat Servicing Unit
FIS	Fighter Instructors School
FRU	Fleet Requirements Unit
FTFlt	Ferry Training Flight
GAL	General Aircraft Ltd (CRO)
GSU	Group Support Unit
HCU	Heavy Conversion Unit
MU	Maintenance Unit
NEA	Non-Effective Airframe
(O)AFU	(Observers) Advanced Flying Unit
OANS	Observers Air Navigation School
OTU	Operational Training Unit
(P)AFU	(Pilots) Advanced Flying Unit
PATP	Packed Aircraft Transit Pool
RAAA	Repaired and Awaiting Allocation
RIW	Repaired in Works
ROS	Repaired on Site
RSU	Repair & Servicing Unit
SAS	Servicing & Aircraft Section
SFTS	Service Flying Training School
SOC	Struck Off Charge

Sqn;Sqd   Squadron
U/S   Unserviceable
WFU   Withdrawn From Use

43 GDA (or variations): 43 (Maintenance) Group 'Disposal Account'
                        - apparently a 'paper' transaction removing an
                        aircraft from a unit's charge whilst it was being
                        modified or repaired

For an explanation of RAF Damage Categories pre-1952, see **Appendix 2**.

Annex 3: RAF Home Commands

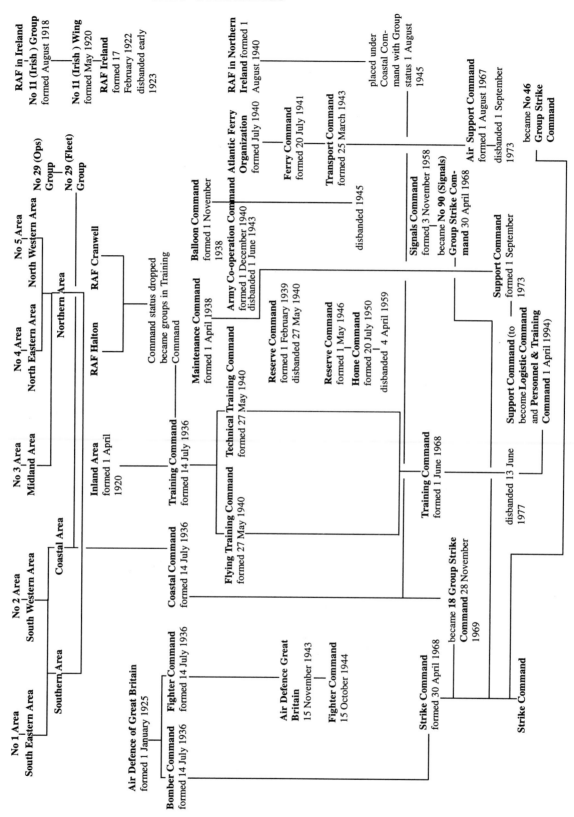

Annex 4: Commissioned Ranks

RNAS 1912-1918

Wing Captain
Wing Commander
Squadron Commander
Flight Lieutenant
Flight Sub-Lieutenant

RFC 1912-1918 & RAF 1918-1919

General
Lieutenant General
Major General
Brigadier
Colonel
Lieutenant Colonel
Major
Captain
Lieutenant
Second Lieutenant

RAF 1919-Present day [2]

Marshal of the Royal Air Force
Air Chief Marshal
Air Marshal
Air Vice-Marshal
Air Commodore
Group Captain
Wing Commander
Squadron Leader
Flight Lieutenant
Flying Officer
Pilot Officer

WAAF & WRAF 1939-1967 [1]

Air Chief Commandant
Air Commandant
Group Officer
Wing Officer
Squadron Officer
Flight Officer
Section Officer [3]
Assistant Section Officer [4]

WRAF 1918-1920

Commandant
Deputy Commandant
Assistant Commandant I
Assistant Commandant II
Administrator
Deputy Administrator
Assistant Administrator

Princess Mary's Royal Air Force Nursing Service [5] **1921-1950**

Matron-in-Chief
Chief Principal Matron [7]
Principal Matron
Matron
Senior Sister
Sister
Staff Nurse [8]

PMRAFNS 1951-1980 [6]

Air Commandant
Group Officer
Wing Officer
Squadron Officer
Flight Officer
Flying Officer

46

1 From 1 August 1968 WRAF officers had the same rank titles as their male counterparts: the WRAF was disbanded in 1994.
2 Introduced 1919 as Marshal of the Air; changed to Marshal of the Royal Air Force in 1925.
3 Changed to Flying Officer in 1949.
4 Changed to Pilot Officer in 1949.
5 Originally the Royal Air Force Nursing Service; became Princess Mary's in 1923.
6 From 1 April 1980, PMRAFNS officers have used the same rank titles as the RAF and WRAF, but the rank of Pilot Officer is not used.
7 In use between March 1944 and July 1948.
8 In use between January 1921 and June 1941.

Annex 5: Non-Commissioned Officers and Airmen/Airwomen

RNAS

Chief Petty Officer I
Chief Petty Officer II
Chief Petty Officer III
Petty Officer
Leading Mechanic
Air Mechanic I
Acting Air Mechanic I
Air Mechanic II

RFC

Warrant Officer
Quartermaster-Sergeant
Flight Sergeant
Sergeant
Corporal
Air Mechanic I
Air Mechanic II
Air Mechanic III

WRAF, 1918-1920

Senior Leader
Chief Section Leader
Section Leader

Sub-Leader

Member

RAF, 1918

Sergeant Major I/Chief Master Mechanic/Chief Master Clerk
Sergeant Major II/Master Mechanic/Master Clerk
Flight Sergeant/Chief Mechanic/Flight Clerk
Sergeant/Sergeant Mechanic/Sergeant Clerk
Corporal/Corporal Mechanic/Corporal Clerk
-    /Air Mechanic 1st Class/Clerk 1st Class
Private 1st Class/Air Mechanic 2nd Class/Clerk 2nd Class
Private 2nd Class/Air Mechanic 3rd Class/Clerk 3rd Class

RAF, 1919-1951[1]

Sergeant Major Class 1[2]
Sergeant Major Class 2[2]
Flight Sergeant
Sergeant
Corporal
Leading Aircraftman
Aircraftman 1st Class
Aircraftman 2nd Class

RAF, 1951-1964[3]

Warrant Officer/Master Technician
Flight Sergeant/Chief Technician[5]
Sergeant/Senior Technician
Corporal/Corporal Technician
Senior Aircraftman/Junior Technician[6]
Leading Aircraftman

RAF, 1964-Date[4]

Warrant Officer/Master Aircrew
Flight Sergeant/Chief Technician[5]
Sergeant
Corporal
Senior Aircraftman/Junior Technician[6]
Leading Aircraftman

48

Aircraftman 1st Class
Aircraftman 2nd Class

-

Aircraftman

PMRAFNS 1963-1971[7]

PMRAFNS 1980-Date[8]

AIRCREW RANKS 1946-1950[9]

Chief Staff Nurse
Senior Staff Nurse
Staff Nurse 1
Staff Nurse
Student Nurse 1
Student Nurse 2
Student Nurse 3

Warrant Officer
Flight Sergeant
Sergeant
Corporal
Senior Aircraftman
Leading Aircraftman
Aircraftman

Master Aircrew
Aircrew I
Aircrew II
Aircrew III / Aircrew IV

1   WAAF and WRAF ranks from 1939 on were similar to the male equivalents, eg Leading Aircraft*woman*.

2   The rank of Sergeant Major was abolished in January 1933 and replaced by a single rank of Warrant Officer.

3   & 4 NCOs and Airmen were placed into trade groups, and the Technician Ranks were linked to trades involving technical skills, such as Engine Fitter and Musician. The traditional ranks were allocated to non-technical trades such as the RAF Regiment, Catering and Supply.

5   Chief Technician is a stage **between** Sergeant and Flight Sergeant.

6   Junior Technician is a stage **between** SAC and Corporal.

7   Before 1963 all members of the PMRAFNS were commissioned. In March 1971 the PMRAFNS ranks were changed to follow the Technician Structure in use at that time for male nurses serving in the RAF. In September of that year the Nursing trade group was split into two parallel schemes: those training as, or qualified as, State Registered Nurses followed the Technician route, whilst men and women qualified as or training as State Enrolled Nurses were allocated the traditional RAF ranks but were unable to rise beyond the rank of Sergeant.

8   From 1 April 1980 all RAF nurses have followed the traditional rank structure.

9   The rank titles used reflected the aircrew specialization, eg Master Pilot, Navigator III, Engineer II, etc. Aircrew under training had the rank of Cadet Pilot, etc. They proved unpopular and were dropped in favour of the Sergeant/Flight Sergeant system, with the exception of Master Aircrew which continues in use.

49

CRANWELL.

Nos. 56, 57, 58.—Training Depôt Stations, etc. (Midland Area ; No. 12 Group, 59th Wing).

LOCATION.—England, Lincolnshire, 14 miles south of Lincoln (pop., 61,000) and 10 miles north-east of Grantham (pop., 20,500). Scopwick Aerodrome is 5 miles to the north and Spittlegate and Harlaxton Aerodromes are 10 and 12 miles to the south-east.

Railway Station :—Caythorpe (G.N. Rly.), 4 miles. There is a railway siding (with station) to the site.

Road :—Main road from Sleaford to Newark passes the site.

FUNCTION.—(*a*) Three Training Depôt Stations of Two Units each for Single Seater Fighter, Day Bombing and Handley-Page training. (*b*) Headquarters of No. 12 Group. (*c*) Headquarters of 59th Wing. (*d*) Wing Aeroplane Repair Section. (*e*) Airship Training Wing. (*f*) Boys' Training Wing. (*g*) Physical Training School. (*h*) Wireless Operators' School. (*j*) Station Establishment.

ESTABLISHMENT.

Personnel.	TDS. S.S.F.	TDS. D.B.	TDS. H.P.	Transport.	TDS. S.S.F.	TDS. D.B.	TDS. H.P.
Officers	34	35		Touring Cars	1	1	
Officers under instruction	80	60		Light Tenders	8	8	
N.C.O.'s under instruction	40	60	Not yet published.	Heavy Tenders	8	8	Not yet published.
W.O.'s and N.C.O.'s above the rank of Corporal	31	33		Motor Cycles	6	6	
Corporals	22	23		Sidecars	4	4	
Rank and File	214	231		Trailers	3	3	
Forewomen	5	5					
Women	105	104					
Women (Household)	42	42					
TOTAL (*exclusive of Hostel Staff*)	573	593		TOTAL	30	30	

Machines.—

Single Seater Fighter. TDS.		Day Bombing. TDS.		Handley-Page. TDS.	
Camel	24	D.H. 4 or 9	24	Handley-Page	8
Avros	24	Avros	24	F.E.	12
				Avros	20
TOTAL	48	TOTAL	48	TOTAL	40

AERODROME.—Maximum dimensions in yards, 4,200 × 2,800. Area, 2,446 acres, of which 300 acres are occupied by the Station Buildings, or are otherwise unavailable for landing. Height above sea level, 150 feet. Soil, a thin layer of loam on limestone. Surface, very good, though it becomes dusty near the sheds. Part of the ground is undulating. A public road and a railway passes across the Aerodrome. The general surroundings are good open undulating country with large fields.

TENURE POLICY.—Not at present on the list of permanent stations.

figure 9: Survey of RAF stations in Britain, 1918: RAF Cranwell (AIR 1/452/15/312/26)

An extract from the quarterly survey of RAF stations in the UK, dated 1918 and showing RAF Cranwell, which was first opened in 1916.

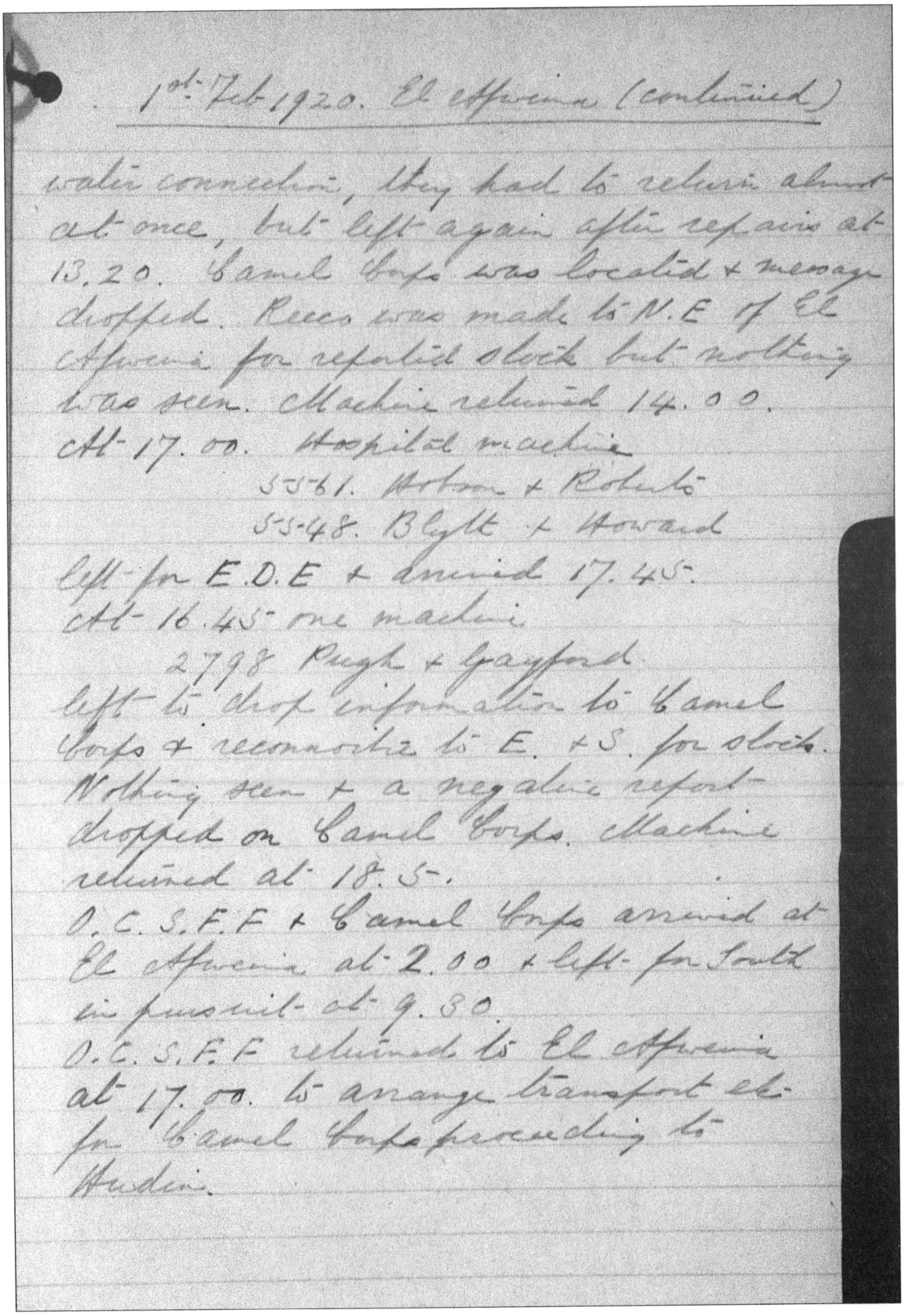

1st Feb 1920. El Afweina (continued)

water connection, they had to return almost
at once, but left again after repairs at
13.20. Camel Corps was located & message
dropped. Recce was made to N.E of El
Afweina for reported stock but nothing
was seen. Machine returned 14.00.
At 17.00. Hospital machine
     5561. Hobson & Roberts
     5548. Blyth & Howard
left for E.D.E & arrived 17.45.
At 16.45 one machine
     2798 Pugh & Gayford
left to drop information to Camel
Corps & reconnoitre to E. & S. for stock.
Nothing seen & a negative report
dropped on Camel Corps. Machine
returned at 18.5.
O.C. S.F.F & Camel Corps arrived at
El Afweina at 2.00 & left for South
in pursuit at 9.30.
O.C. S.F.F returned to El Afweina
at 17.00. to arrange transport etc.
for Camel Corps proceeding to
Hudin.

figure 10: War Diary for 'Z' unit in British Somaliland, 1 February 1920 (AIR 5/1309)

Part of the record book of the RAF's 'Z' Force, consisting of twelve Airco DH9s, which in January 1920 was shipped to British Somaliland in HMS *Ark Royal* to help subdue a bandit known as 'The Mad Mullah' who had increased his raiding activities during the First World War. Between 21 January and 9 February 1920, bombing by these aircraft destroyed the Mullah's forts and the campaign was over.

figure 11: Fairey Flycatcher arcraft, 1923 (AIR 5/240)

The Fairey Flycatcher single-seat fighter served with the Fleet Air Arm on aircraft carriers from 1923 to 1934, serial N163 in this photograph being the first of three prototypes. The aircraft was unusual since the wings did not fold, but the airframe could be dismantled easily for stowage. The upswept underside of the fuselage and the large wheels gave a rather strange appearance to the aircraft in flight. The Flycatcher could also be fitted with floats for amphibian operations.

figure 12: R101 airship, 1930 (AIR 5/919)

The airship R101, 777 feet long, at her mooring mast at the Royal Airship Works in Cardington. She was ready to fly in October 1929 and, after test flights, left Cardington on 4 October 1930 for Karachi.

figure 13: Supermarine S6B, 1931 (INF 2/3, p 30)

Supermarine S6B serial S1595, the high-speed seaplane which was flown by Flt Lt J N Boothman to win first place in the twelfth Schneider Trophy contest held in the Solent on 12 September 1931. This gave the RAF its third successive win in the competition, thus gaining the trophy in perpetuity. On 29 September 1931, this machine was flown by Flt Lt G H Stainforth at 407.5mph to give Britain the World Speed Record. The experience gained with the Supermarine racing seaplanes had an important influence on the design of the Spitfire. The seaplane in this photograph is on public display at the Science Museum in London.

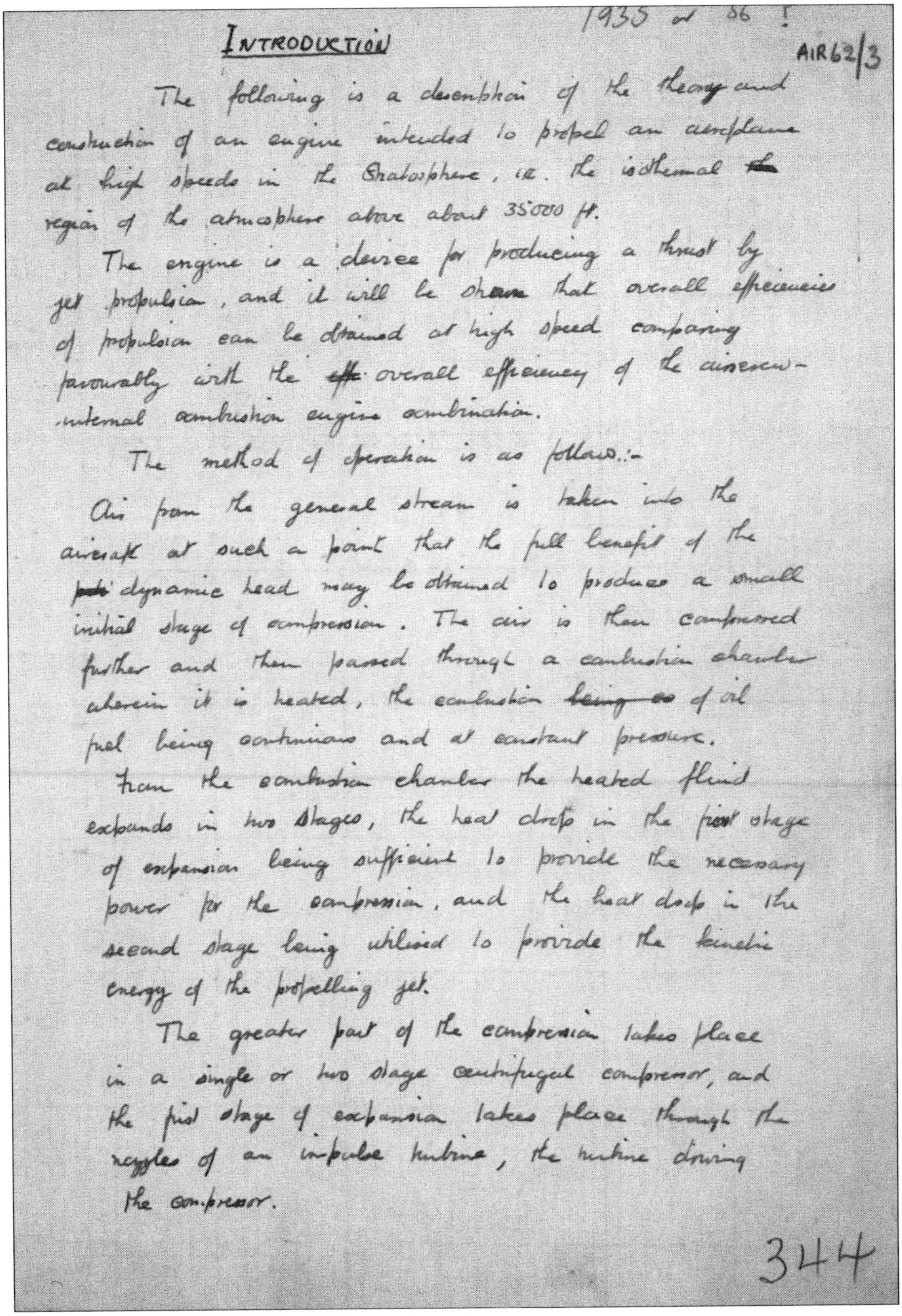

INTRODUCTION

The following is a description of the theory and construction of an engine intended to propel an aeroplane at high speeds in the Stratosphere, i.e. the isothermal ~~the~~ region of the atmosphere above about 35,000 ft.

The engine is a device for producing a thrust by jet propulsion, and it will be shown that overall efficiencies of propulsion can be obtained at high speed comparing favourably with the ~~eff.~~ overall efficiency of the airscrew-internal combustion engine combination.

The method of operation is as follows :-

Air from the general stream is taken into the aircraft at such a point that the full benefit of the ~~pot.~~ dynamic head may be obtained to produce a small initial stage of compression. The air is then compressed further and then passed through a combustion chamber wherein it is heated, the combustion ~~being as~~ of oil fuel being continuous and at constant pressure.

From the combustion chamber the heated fluid expands in two stages, the heat drop in the first stage of expansion being sufficient to provide the necessary power for the compression, and the heat drop in the second stage being utilised to provide the kinetic energy of the propelling jet.

The greater part of the compression takes place in a single or two stage centrifugal compressor, and the first stage of expansion takes place through the nozzles of an impulse turbine, the turbine driving the compressor.

344

figure 14: Notebook of Fl Lt Frank Whittle on the theory of the jet engine, 1935 or 1936 (AIR 62/3)

Part of a notebook kept by Flt Lt Frank Whittle on the theory of the jet engine, written in 1935 or 1936.

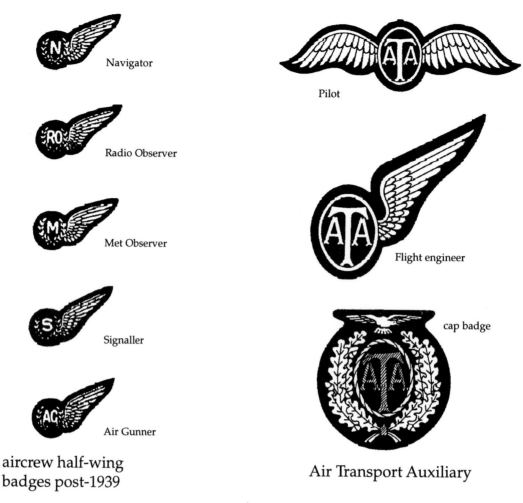

Navigator

Radio Observer

Met Observer

Signaller

Air Gunner

aircrew half-wing
badges post-1939

Pilot

Flight engineer

cap badge

Air Transport Auxiliary

shoulder title

Ground Gunner

Signaller arm badge

Aden Protectorate Levies

parachute wings

RAF Regiment badges of 1942

Service badges of the Second World War

SECTION THREE
The Second World War
by
Roy Conyers Nesbit

Records of the RAF's part in the Second World War became steadily more voluminous in the course of the war, but the accuracy and contents in the early years varied considerably. This is particularly true of the Squadron and Station Operations Record Books, which depended on the diligence of those compiling the records and the opportunity presented for writing them.

As in all large organizations, the route taken by written communications in the RAF in the Second World War was determined by the pattern under which authority was delegated. That pattern was established in a reorganization which took place in 1936, and it was under this revised structure that wartime activities were carried out. This part of the guide starts by describing sources of recorded information by reference to that structure. It continues by indicating where particular records are most likely to be found in the PRO.

Many researchers wish to find out as much as possible about a particular RAF operation. These records can vary from a brief entry in a single document to those where entries can be found under numerous lettercodes, classes and piece numbers. One example of an operation where there are numerous pieces is the famous dam-busting operation by the Lancasters of 617 Squadron on the night of 16/17 May 1943, as listed in the **Examples of research** section below. Other examples of types of research are also given in that section.

Central direction of policy

The War Cabinet, established in September 1939, met daily for most of the early period, supported on the military side by the Chiefs of Staff Committee which advised on defence policy, as well as other committees on a permanent or an ad hoc basis. Policy matters which affected the RAF can be found in the following:

CAB 65   War Cabinet Minutes and conclusions from Sept 1939 to May 1945, with a subject index in Ledger 55.

CAB 66   War Cabinet Memoranda in the WP and CP Series. In date order only, without subject index.

CAB 67   War Cabinet Memoranda in the WP (G) Series. In date order only, without subject index.

CAB 68   War Cabinet Memoranda in the WP (R) Series. In date order only, without subject index.

CAB 69   War Cabinet Defence Committee (Operations). In date order only, without subject index.

CAB 70   War Cabinet Defence Committee (Supply). In date order only, with out subject index.

CAB 78   War Cabinet Committees, MISC and GEN Series. In date order, but with subjects also listed.

CAB 83   War Cabinet Ministerial Committee on Military Co-ordination. In date order only, without subject index.

CAB 84   Joint Planning Committees. In date order only, without subject index.

CAB 85   War Cabinet Anglo-French Committees, with minutes and meetings of the various Anglo-French Liaison and Co-ordinating Committees on military matters. In date order, but with subjects also listed.

CAB 88   War Cabinet Combined Chiefs of Staff Committee and Sub-Committees. In date order only, without subject index.

CAB 92   War Cabinet Committees on Supply, Production, Priority and Manpower. In date order, but with subjects listed.

CAB 93   War Cabinet Home Defence Committee. In date order, but with subjects listed.

CAB 94   War Cabinet Overseas Defence Committee. In date order only.

CAB 95   War Cabinet Committees on the Middle East and Africa. In date order, but with subjects also listed.

CAB 96   War Cabinet Committees on the Far East. In date order, but with subjects also listed.

CAB 98   War Cabinet Miscellaneous Committees, including military matters. In date order, but with subjects also listed.

CAB 100   War Cabinet daily situation reports, in the Central War Room. In date order only.

CAB 105   War Cabinet telegrams sent to overseas Commands. In date order, but with destinations listed.

When Winston S Churchill replaced Neville Chamberlain as Prime Minister on 11 May 1940, he also assumed the title of Minister of Defence. The scope and powers of this office were not defined, nor was a Ministry created. Churchill required only what he termed a 'handling machine', and the military wing of the War Cabinet fulfilled that function. Policy matters relating to the RAF can be found in the following:

CAB 120   This contains the files of the Secretariat of the Minister of Defence and includes details of Prime Minister's intervention in operational matters, listed firstly under Royal Air Force and then under subjects.

PREM 3   Similar papers can be found under Prime Minister's Office: Operational Papers. These are indexed alphabetically under, for example, Air, Radio Direction Finding, German Air Force, Bombs, Prisoners of War, Bombsights, War, etc.

PREM 4   Other papers of a similar nature, under Confidential Papers. These are also indexed alphabetically under, for example, Air, War, etc.

The Air Ministry was the civilian body which governed the RAF, which in turn operated under a comand structure reorganized in 1936 and continued with little change throughout the war. The highest power was vested in the Air Council, with the Secretary of State for Air as president. Under him came the Parliamentary Under-Secretary, the Chief of the Air Staff, the Vice-Chief of the Air Staff and three Air Members (for Personnel, Supply and Training), the Permanent Under-Secretary, and various additional members whose posts varied in the course of the war. Some documents are listed under the names of those who occupied the highest positions during the Second World War, such as the Secretaries of State for Air and the Chiefs of Air Staff. The names of the Chiefs of Air Staff are shown in **Appendix 1**.

The members of the Air Staff were the Vice-Chief, the Deputy-Chief and assistant Chiefs for various matters. These members controlled various Directorates, such as those of Plans, Operational Requirements (Home, Overseas and Naval Co-operation), Intelligence, Allied Co-operation, Ground Defence and Signals. The Directorate were given the responsibility of assembling and studying information in their designated fields. During the course of the war new Directorates were created or disbanded when outmoded.

Below the Air Staff, the RAF was organized in functional Commands within the United Kingdom and geographical Commands overseas, with the operational chain of authority passing to the Commanders in Chief of these Commands.

Within the Air Ministry business was conducted on registered files controlled by a Central Registry, but as the war developed its various branches also began to maintain their own unregistered files. The files relating to policy can be found in the following:

AIR 2   This class list contains so many items of registered correspondence that it is in sixteen Volumes. These are in two sections:
                     Code A contains many matters prior to the Second World War.
                     Code B concentrates on matters during the Second World War.
             The files of correspondence under each code have been grouped under subject headings (and sub-headings) conforming to the code system used in the Air Ministry Registry. A list of subject headings is given for each Code, such as:
                     Accidents
                     Aircraft
                     Engines
                     Meteorology
                     Radar
                     WAAF
             One Volume contains a 'Packing List' (the binder is clearly labelled) which lists cross-references with the reference numbers given to the documents by the Air Historical Branch of the Ministry of Defence before they were transferred to the Public Record Office. This Packing List is in the PRO's numerical order, so that trying to find a piece number from an original reference could be lengthy work.

AIR 6   Contains records of meetings of the Air Council. This class also contains minutes and memoranda submitted to the Secretary of State for Air concerning plans for expansion of the RAF in 1940. These records are in date order only.

AIR 8   Contains records formerly in the office of the Chief of the Air Staff. This class includes reports and policies relating to all aspects of the conduct of the war. There is a subject index in alphabetical order covering numerous subjects, such as:
                     Accidents: prevention: flying
                     Aircrews: Chances of survival

Airfields: Construction of
American Air Forces: Orders of Battle
Anti-submarine campaign
Army: air support for
Bomber Command: operations
Flying bombs: fighter defence against
Italy: air operations against
Japan: Air Forces for
Malta: 'Torch' operations from
Minelaying: by aircraft
Navy: air co-operation with
Night air defence: use of 'window' for
Pathfinder Force: formation
Russia: aircraft supplies
South-East Asia: operations
Training: expansion of
Transport Command: formation of

AIR 9   Contains records of the Director of Plans under the Assistant Chief of the Air Staff. This class is indexed alphabetically and includes such matters as the strategic planning of operations in the Mediterranean, Italy and South-East Asia, and the strategy of the Joint Planning Staff.

AIR 10   Air Publications produced by the Air Ministry. This is a very large class, and those records which relate to the Second World War are contained within pieces 1-5837. There is a key to the arrangement whereby Codes are given to various headings and sub-headings such as:

	Code
<u>Administration and Training</u> Training: Flying Training	1/6
<u>Armament</u> Guns and Gun Sights	2/2
<u>Engineering</u> Aero-engines (by name)	3/3
<u>Signals</u> Radar Equipment (Airborne)	6/5

> Airfield Construction
> Earth-boring Equipment   8/12

AIR 19   Contains Private Office Papers of the Secretary of State for Air and
           the Under-Secretary of State for Air. These are arranged in date or
           der but with a brief description of contents, such as Air Bases, Ferry
           Pilots, Bombing of German Targets, Casualties, Air Attacks on
           Shipping, etc.

AIR 20   Contains unregistered Papers from the various branches of the Air
           Ministry. These cover similar subjects to those in AIR 2, but were not
           registered by the Air Ministry. The class list is in four volumes:
           In Volume 1:
                   Pieces 1-762 contain mainly pre-war documents and have a
                   geographical index.
                   Pieces 763-6285 relate to the Second World War, with a subject
                   index containing such subjects as:
                           Bomber Operations: Directorate of
                           British Bombing Research Mission
                           Directorate of Operations (Air Defence)
                           Directorate of Operations (Training)
           Volumes 2-4 relate mostly to the period after 1945.

AIR 42   Combined Operational Planning Committee. The pieces in this class
           relate to a committee set up in June 1943, staffed by RAF and United
           States Army Air Force (USAAF) personnel, with the main objective
           of co-ordinating the strategic bombing campaign against Germany
           and German-occupied Europe. It also includes some appreciations
           of the strength of German fighter defences.

Commands

The Headquarters of most major Commands consisted of an Air Officer Commander in Chief supported by a Senior Air Staff Officer on the operational side and an Air Officer in charge of administration, together with other officers responsible for specialized duties. Records of the various Commands, providing sources for the planning and conduct of operations, can be found in the classes listed below. Within the class list, the pieces are listed in PRO classification order, often without any alphabetical or logical sequence. You may expect a fairly prolonged task in hunting for any particular subject in some of them.

AIR 13   Balloon Command. Files relating to organization, barrages, equipment, operations, etc. This command, which was formed in 1938, came under the operational control of the headquarters of Fighter Command at Stanmore in Middlesex.

AIR 14   Bomber Command. This is a voluminous class, containing files of headquarters Bomber Command and some of its groups, relating to planning, tactics, crews, equipment, etc.

The Command was responsible for the strategic employment of bomber Squadrons based within the United Kingdom, with headquarters at High Wycombe in Buckinghamshire. In the early years of the war, its broad strategy was decided by the Chief of the Air Staff in consultation with the Defence Committee, the Chiefs of Staff Committee, the Ministry of Economic Warfare and with the Allies. This system was modified in June 1943 when a Combined Operational Planning Committee was established to co-ordinate the strategic bombing operations of Bomber Command and the United States Eighth Air Force based in Britain, supported by escorting aircraft of Fighter Command (see also AIR 42 above).

In the middle of 1944, a Joint Target Priorities Committee was also set up to decide which targets should be attacked to counter German flying bombs and rockets; the members were representatives of the Air Ministry and the USAAF.

AIR 15   Coastal Command. The pieces in this class include files of Headquarters Coastal Command at Northwood in Middlesex, relating to such subjects as organization, planning, exercises, tactics, protection of shipping, anti-submarine operations, minelaying, attacks on enemy shipping, etc.

The role of this Command at the outbreak of war was the exercise of air power around the coasts of Britain, but in January 1941 units were established in Iceland and in December of that year RAF Gibraltar was also placed under its control. The Azores were added in October 1943. In June 1940 the Photographic Reconnaissance Unit operating from the United Kingdom came under its control and Air-Sea Rescue was added in August 1941. In the course of the war, special Strike Wings were formed to attack enemy coastal trade around the coasts of North-West Europe.

From its formation before the war, the function of this Command was trade protection, reconnaissance and co-operation with the Royal Navy but in April 1941 operational control was passed to the Admiralty. The staff officers at Coastal Command took this to mean that the Admiralty had the right to indicate to their Commander the lines along which operations should be directed, without weakening his responsibility to the Chiefs of Air Staff for the conduct of his Command. Thus some research into Coastal Command activities might involve some reference to Admiralty papers relating to policy, but all operational flying records are in the AIR classes.

AIR 16   Fighter Command. Files of Headquarters Fighter Command at Stanmore relating to organization, defence schemes, trials, training, etc.

The primary responsibility of this Command was the air defence of the United Kingdom, as exemplified by the Battle of Britain in the late summer of 1940, but encounters also took place over enemy territory. The first major air battles outside the UK occurred in May 1940, during the German Blitzkrieg in the West. From late 1940 onwards RAF fighters began to escort bombers in offensive operations over France, Belgium and Holland.

In its defensive role, the Command exercised control over the Army's Anti-Aircraft Command and the RAF's Balloon Command, as well as the radar chain around British shores and the Observer Corps. In November 1943 this Command was renamed Air Defence of Great Britain while it formed part of the Allied Expeditionary Force for the invasion of Europe, but the title of Fighter Command was restored after almost a year.

AIR 17   Maintenance Command. A number of files relating to the formation, organization and activities of Maintenance Command, which carried out storage, servicing and repair functions. The headquarters of this Command, which was formed in 1938, were at Abingdon in Oxfordshire.

AIR 23   Overseas Commands. This is a very large class of records of RAF Commands, Air Forces and other units based in the Mediterranean, Middle East (including Iraq and Aden), India and South-East Asia. Overseas Commands, which were responsible directly to the Air Staff, were organized on a geographical basis, each with its own fighter, bomber and maritime Squadrons, as well as its own organizations for repair and maintenance.

There is a subject index to the Commands, etc covered by this class, the entries relating mainly to geographical areas such as:
Aden
Gibraltar
Malta
Middle East
Western Desert

AIR 32   Training Command. A small number of Second World War files relating to flying training, technical training, the medical aspects of flying training, and the training of special agents for clandestine operations. Most of the documents in this class are post-war, however.

AIR 38   Ferry and Transport Commands. Records of the Atlantic Ferry Organization (ATFERO), formed in 1940 as a civilian organization under the organization of the Ministry of Aircraft Production for ferrying aircraft from the USA and Canada to Britain; of Ferry Command which succeeded ATFERO in July 1941; and of Transport Command which took over the functions of Ferry Command in March 1943. Examples of files are Catalina Deliveries to Russia, the Azores Staging Post, BOAC Air Routes, Iceland and Trooping by Air.

AIR 39   Army Co-operation Command. Files relating to this Command from the time it was formed on 1 December 1940 to the time it was absorbed by the Tactical Air Force on 1 June 1943. Examples of files are those concerning Aircraft Tugs, Gliders, the Raid on Bruneval in February 1942, Airborne Forces, the RAF Regiment and Paratroop Aircraft.

Expeditions

AIR 35   British Air Forces in France. Surviving records from September 1939 to May 1940. Most of the records concern administration and strategic matters but there are also some intelligence reports.

AIR 36   Air Component North West Expeditionary Force (Norway). The few surviving records of the expedition in April 1940 until the evacuation the following month, mostly of an operational nature.

AIR 37   Allied Expeditionary Air Force (AEAF). Extensive Records of the AEAF, which took part in the invasion of Europe from June 1944, and its principal components the RAF's 2nd Tactical Air Force (2nd TAF) and the USAAF'S 9th Air Force. There are also files originating at Supreme Headquarters Allied Expeditionary Force (SHAEF). The files are arranged firstly with a Packing List giving the piece numbers in numerical order, then a Contents List giving the piece numbers under headings, and finally a more detailed descriptive list. As examples, under SHAEF (Main and Rear) there are Operation 'Crossbow', Operation 'Overlord', Employment of Air Forces, Supply by Air, Relief Food Supplies for the Dutch; under Allied Expeditionary Air Force, there are 2nd TAF Formation and Organization, Operation 'Varsity', Glider Raid Reports, SAS Operation 'Sunflower'.

AIR 47   Operation Torch: Planning Papers. The Planning and organization for the British air element in Operation 'Torch', the Allied invasion of North Africa in November 1942, was carried out by 333 Group, later Eastern Air Command. You should note that the operational papers of Eastern Air Command are in AIR 23.

Missions and delegations

AIR 33   RAF Inspectorate General. The Inspector was responsible for inspecting units of the RAF and WAAF. This class contains reports of visits, including some to units of the RAAF.

AIR 45   RAF Delegation, Washington. This began in June 1941, while the USA was still neutral. The pieces in this class relate to allocation of air craft, the training of RAF personnel in North America and liaison with the US Army and Navy Air Forces. They also include a series on air-sea rescue techniques and equipment.

AIR 46   Records of the Air Liaison Missions to Canada, South Africa, Egypt and the USSR. They cover the Empire Air Training Schemes, the training of the Royal Norwegian Air Force in Canada, and the escape of PoWs from enemy-held territory.

Operations Record Books (ORBs)

These records are probably consulted more often than any others in the AIR classes. Entries are on two RAF forms:

Forms 540 for monthly summaries, by Commands, Groups, Wings, Squadrons and smaller units.

Forms 541 for daily details, mostly kept by Squadrons. In the early days of the war, the accuracy and content of these reports varied considerably, depending on the person allocated for this duty.

In addition ORBs are sometimes accompanied by Appendixes which can include important details, and you are advised not to miss these.

AIR 24 Commands. Forms 540 and Appendixes arranged under each Command or Force. There is an alphabetical index with headings such as:

> Balkan Air Force
> Bomber Command
> Coastal Command
> Desert Air Force
> Ferry Command
> Fighter Command
> Gibraltar Command
> India Command
> Maintenance Command
> Women's Auxiliary Air Force

There are numerous pieces under some of these headings and you may expect a lengthy hunt when looking for a particular subject.

AIR 25 Groups. Forms 540 and Appendixes indexed numerically for each Group in the Commands, including all those which came under Bomber, Fighter, Coastal, India, RCAF, Training, Army Co-operation, Ferry, Maintenance, Signals, Balloon Barrage, Airborne Forces, etc.

AIR 26 Wings. Forms 540 and Appendixes for all Wings, indexed numerically under titles such as Indian, Signals, Fighter, Coastal, Bomber, Base Defence, Army Co-operation, Maintenance, General Reconnaissance, Photographic Reconnaissance, Transport, Tactical, Special Duty, etc.

AIR 27 Squadrons. Most of these consist of Forms 540 and Forms 541, sometimes with separate Appendixes, and are indexed numerically under the Squadron number. They vary considerably in details, according to the time allocated to writing them, sometimes in difficult circumstances, but generally become more comprehensive after the first two years of the war. Records of those Squadrons which flew in the Battle of Britain are sometimes scrappy. Sections of the records of some Squadrons are missing entirely, for example those which served in Malta during the time the island came under continual air attack.

You should note that the times of take-off and landing of aircraft based in the UK can vary from local time to Greenwich Mean Time (GMT), and that it is sometimes difficult to distinguish which were entered in the records. Generally times were recorded in local time, but where they were taken from navigators' logs in Squadrons based in the UK, they were usually in GMT.

During the war, local time varied from GMT to British Summer Time (BST, 1 hour in advance of GMT) to British Double Summer Time (BDST, 2 hours in advance of GMT). An example of this difference in times is:

GMT		BST		BDST
14.00 hrs	=	15.00 hrs	=	16.00 hrs

Local time in the UK varied as follows:

From	02.00 hrs Sunday	16 Apr 1939	- BST
"	02.00 hrs "	19 Nov 1939	- GMT
"	02.00 hrs "	25 Feb 1940	- BST
"	02.00 hrs "	4 May 1941	- BDST
"	02.00 hrs "	10 Aug 1941	- BST
"	02.00 hrs "	5 Apr 1942	- BDST
"	02.00 hrs "	9 Aug 1942	- BST
"	02.00 hrs "	4 Apr 1943	- BDST
"	02.00 hrs "	15 Aug 1943	- BST
"	02.00 hrs "	2 Apr 1944	- BDST
"	02.00 hrs "	17 Sept 1944	- BST
"	02.00 hrs Monday	2 Apr 1945	- BDST
"	02.00 hrs Sunday	15 July 1945	- BST
"	02.00 hrs "	7 Oct 1945	- GMT

On the other hand, the Germans used Central European Time (CET, 1 hour in advance of GMT) and German Summer Time (GST, 2 hours in advance of GMT), so that for example:

GMT		CET		GST
14.00 hrs	=	15.00 hrs	=	16.00 hrs

Local time in the Germany varied as follows:

To	02.00 hrs Monday		1 Apr 1940	- CET
From	02.00 hrs	"	1 Apr 1940	- GST
				(then all 1941)
"	02.00 hrs	"	2 Nov 1942	- CET
"	02.00 hrs	"	29 Mar 1943	- GST
"	02.00 hrs	"	4 Oct 1943	- CET
"	02.00 hrs	"	3 Apr 1944	- GST
"	02.00 hrs	"	2 Oct 1944	- CET
"	02.00 hrs	"	2 Apr 1945	- GST
"	02.00 hrs Sunday		18 Nov 1945	- CET

The Italian forces, collaborating with the Germans from the time their country entered the war on 10 June 1940 to the Armistice with the Allies on 7 September 1943, also conformed with German times.

A further compliction in this class can arise in methods of reporting position. Maritime Squadrons often used codes issued to the Royal Navy and the Fleet Air Arm, wherein lines of latitude and longitude were each given two code letters. The method of reporting position was first to give the code letters denoting the degrees of latitude and longitude immediately to the <u>south and west</u> of the required point, and then to give the distance in minutes of latitude and minutes of longitude from this intersection. Thus if $50°$ N was represented by AB and $23°$ W by XY, then the position $50°$ 08'N $22°$ 33'W was denoted by ABXY 0827. This method remained the same whether the position was east or west of the Greewich meridian or north or south of the Equator. Moreover, the code letters changed periodically. These codes are being transferred to ADM 186 from the Naval Historical Branch (NHB).

AIR 28   Stations. There are Forms 540 and Appendixes for the main RAF Stations throughout all the theatres of war. The stations are not arranged in strict alphabetical order but they are grouped under their initial letters and there is also an alphabetical index. This class in cludes training Stations as well as operational.

AIR 29   Miscellaneous Units. This is a very large class containing Forms 540 and Appendixes for units other than Commands, Groups, Wings, Squadrons and Stations. There are two indexes, by place names and by types of units such as:

       Advanced Flying Boat Bases

        Air Sea Rescue Units
        Balloon Centres
        Demobilization Centre
        Elementary Flying Training Schools
        Ground Combat Training Schools
        Maintenance Units
        RAF Regiment Squadrons
        WAAF Recruitment Centres

AIR 54   South African Air Force. Microfilm copies of records, some of which are also in AIR 24 Commands, AIR 25 Groups, AIR 26 Wings, AIR 27 Squadrons, AIR 28 Stations and AIR 29 Miscellaneous Units.

Intelligence

Although some aspects of intelligence can be found in many of the classes listed above, the following are devoted primarily to this subject:

AIR 22   Periodical Returns, Summaries and Bulletins. This class contains information provided to the Air Ministry War Room. It includes daily summaries of operations, daily reports of enemy air activity, daily weather summaries and returns of operational Squadrons and crews. Some of these reports were filed a day or two after the event, particularly where the information was received from Overseas Commands. They can provide a very useful general background to detailed research into any particular RAF operation.

AIR 34   Photographic Intelligence. Interpretation reports, usually based on photographs taken by reconnaissance aircraft, covering Germany, Occupied Europe, Italy, Middle East, Far East, the Mediterranean, etc. Some records are arranged under units, such as the Allied Central Interpretation Unit, the Photo Intelligence Centre (Fifth Army), etc, and then in date order. Others are listed under the headings of Germany, Holland and Poland. This class also includes the original photographs included in the publication 'Evidence in Camera' issued by the Joint School of Photographic Interpretation from October 1942 to March 1945.

AIR 40   Directorate of Intelligence and other intelligence papers. This contains a subject index with entries such as Changi PoW Camp, Pathfinder Force, Mediterranean Tactical Air Force, but you will probably find it necessary to check through all the subjects listed against the numerical piece numbers, since these cover such a very wide field. For example, under Air Intelligence 1(a) there are reports on returned RAF, RCAF and RAAF prisoners of war; under Air Intelligence 2(g) there are reports on enemy aircrafts and engines; under Air Intelligence 2(b) there are lists of airfields in enemy territory; under Air Intelligence 3(USA) there are reports, analyses and narratives of the US Eighth Air Force; under Air Intelligence 3(e) there are assessments of the German Air Force. Many other intelligence reports can be found in this class.

AIR 48   United States Strategic Bombing Survey. This was set up by the United States Secretary of War on 3 November 1944, with headquarters in London, to examine the effects of the bombing campaign against Germany. The survey team entered Germany in April 1945 and carried out most of its research during the remainder of that year, although it was not allowed to enter the Russian Zone. In late 1945 most of the team was withdrawn to Washington and subsequently made a similar study of the effects of the war against Japan. This class contains reports of the bombing of particular industries and factories in Germany and German-occupied territory, as well as Japan. Reports on the effect of the atomic bombs dropped on Nagasaki and Hiroshima are also included.

AIR 52   United States National Defence Research Committee. Contains a number of studies and reports on such subject as:
    Co-operative study of area bombing
    Economic consequences of 'mass' attacks on Japanese Cities
    High level and medium level bridge bombing
    Measurement of underwater explosion pressures
    Survey of effectiveness of bombing of invasion coast defences
        on D-Day
    Theory and practice of incendiary bombing

Women in the RAF and ATA

The Women's Auxiliary Air Force (WAAF) was formed in June 1939, and the young recruits began to take over some of the duties hitherto carried out by men. By the outbreak of the war the force numbered 8000 women and then it expanded at an enormous rate, the range of duties being steadily expanded although these remained non-combatant. Air Ministry correspondence relating to the WAAF can be found in AIR 2 (Codes 77/1 and 77/2), and the ORBs of the Directorate of the WAAF at the Air Ministry are in AIR 24/1640-1646. Women were frequently employed as photo-interpreters; their reports are in AIR 34, but these were not signed for security reasons. Otherwise, the majority of the records of the WAAF are included with those of the units in which they served, such as AIR 28 and AIR 29 Stations. WAAF Recruitment Centres are also in AIR 29.

Women also played an important part, together with men, as experienced pilots in the Air Transport Auxiliary (ATA). This was a civilian organization formed in February 1940 and administered by the British Airways Corporation. Its main function was the ferrying of aircraft from the factory to units of the RAF and the Fleet Air Arm. Records of the ATA relating to its formation, recruitment, operations and winding up in November 1945 can be found in AVIA 27. Other files relating to its establishment can be found in AIR 2 (Code 22). ATA personal files were presented by the MOD to the RAF Museum.

Individual records

AIR 4   Flying Log Books. A selection of aircrew's Flying Log Books, containing a record of all flights made, listed under surnames. There are some famous names, such as Wg Cdr B E Finucane and Wg Cdr G P Gibson, but others are those who flew on less well known duties such as air-sea rescue, ferrying, training, etc.

AIR 30   Submission papers. Submissions to the Sovereign for royal approval of appointments, awards and regulations, and petitions in court martial cases. Many of these pieces concern honorary appointments in the RAF for those who served the Royal Household.

AIR 50   Combat Reports. Most are listed under headings such as Fighter Command, Bomber Command, Coastal Command, Fleet Air Arm, United States Air Force, etc, and then under Squadron numbers. Others are listed under High-ranking Officers, Fighter Wings or Miscellaneous Units and Flights. The reports include those of several Battle of Britain pilots, but you should note that not all Combat Reports have survived.

Awards for gallantry and meritorious service

The RAF's four awards for gallantry were the Distinguished Flying Cross, the Distinguished Flying Medal, the Air Force Cross and the Air Force Medal. These were of two types, immediate and non-immediate. In exceptional circumstances, personnel in the RAF and those in the Dominion Air Forces could also receive gallantry awards which normally applied to other branches of the armed services, such as the Military Cross and the Military Medal. In addition, they could be awarded medals which applied to all branches of the service, such as the Victoria Cross, the Order of the British Empire and the Distinguished Service Order, as well as those medals which were instituted primarily for civilian acts of gallantry, such as the George Cross and the George Medal.

Awards were frequently noted in Squadron ORBs under AIR 27 or in Station ORBs under AIR 28 or AIR 29. Most notifications of awards for gallantry and meritorious service were published in the monthly *London Gazette* which can be found, together with indexes, in ZJ 1. It should be noted, however, that there was always a delay between the receipt of an award and its notification in a *Gazette*. Surviving recommendations for awards can be found under AIR 2 Code No 30, but when searching for an you award must expect a long hunt in numerous pieces unless you know the theatre of war and the date when the recommendation is likely to have been made.

There are no medal rolls for campaign medals during the Second World War.

Crashes and casualties

Details of the losses of aircraft and aircrews can usually be found in ORBs for Squadrons under AIR 27 and for Stations under AIR 28 and AIR 29. However, these seldom contain information concerning the fate of crews who failed to return from operations over enemy territory. Such information is held by the AHB, but is not available for general inspection.

The ledger *RAF War Dead 1939-48* at the General Register Office at St Catherine's House in London gives names, ranks, service numbers and units of all RAF personnel who lost their lives outside the shores of the United Kingdom. However, this ledger does not include those who were killed within the country, nor does it include the Dominion Air Forces unless the personnel served in the RAF.

Full names of all British Empire and Commonwealth air personnel who lost their lives during both the First and the Second World Wars are to be found in ledgers in the RAF Church of St Clement Dane's in Aldwych, but these records do not include ranks, service numbers or units.

The Commonwealth War Graves Commission may be able to give information such as unit, date of death and next of kin.

From January 1943 aircraft lost by Bomber Command are noted in AIR 14/2791 Missing Aircraft Register. Other sources are in AIR 14/3466-3473, which contain 'K' reports submitted by survivors of bomber crews on the circumstances in which their aircraft were lost on operations. AIR 14/3213-3227 Raid Plots contain visual reports by returning aircrews of other aircraft seen to be under attack or to have crashed, usually on night operations; these reports are often accompanied by positions marked on charts.

RAF aircraft lost in accidents were recorded on Air Ministry Form 1180. These are held by the Air Historical Branch (AHB), with microfilm copies at the Royal Air Force Museum. The forms are arranged under type of aircraft and date of loss, and usually include brief summaries of the findings of Courts of Inquiry. Ministry of Defence regulations prohibit photocopying but you can make transcripts.

The results of detailed investigations into crashed German aircraft are to be found in Fighter Command AIR 16/166-173, in Periodical Returns AIR 22/266 and 267, and in Directorate of Intelligence AIR 40/45 and AIR 40/1166.

Prisoners in enemy hands

Information regarding British and Allied airmen who fell into enemy hands can be found in the following:

AIR 2 Code 89	This concerns registered correspondence of the Air Ministry on the subject, including such matters as:
	    Repatriation of PoWs in German hands
	    PoWs in Germany and Italy: payment to officers
	    RAF prison camps in Germany: reports
	    Court of inquiry: killing of fifty RAF officers from Stalag Luft III

AIR 14/353-361	These deal mainly with aids to escape and conduct in enemy territory.
AIR 14/461-465	These contain details of German camps and interrogation methods.
AIR 14/469-471	These contain reports of many RAF servicemen taken prisoner in occupied Europe, giving details of their capture.

AIR 14/1233	This also contains reports from RAF PoWs.
AIR 14/1235-1240	These give location lists of PoW camps in Germany, Italy and occupied Europe, together with some aerial photographs.
AIR 20 Code 89	This concerns unregistered correspondence of the Air Ministry about PoWs, including such subjects as:

Nuremberg trials: purported notes by Air Ministry historian

Reports of RAF escapers and evaders

RAF PoWs in Far East: report by Air Commodore Modin

AIR 20/2336	This gives an alphabetical list of all RAF and Dominion Air Force PoWs in German hands in 1944-1945, showing ranks, service numbers and the camps in which they were held.
AIR 40/227-231	These give Air Intelligence on Allied PoW camps in Holland and Germany, together with some photographs.
AIR 40/1488-1491	These contain nominal rolls of prisoners in Stalag Luft III and Stalag IIIA, together with recommendations for meritorious service. Stalag Luft III was the camp from which seventy-six RAF officers escaped in March 1944, fifty of whom were later shot and killed on Hitler's orders.
AIR 40/1545-1552	These contain reports of RAF and Dominion Air Force escapers.
AIR 40/2361	These contain details of conditions of German PoW camps and treatment of prisoners.
AIR 40/2366	These contain details of conditions in Japanese PoW camps and treatment of prisoners.
AIR 49/383-388	These concern nominal rolls for individual camps, principally Japanese, prepared post-war for medical and historical purposes.

Courts Martial

Almost all documents relating to courts martial proceedings during the Second World War are closed for fifty or seventy-five years. Some 'out-letter' books from the Judge Advocate General's Office are available in AIR 71, but the proceedings of the courts martial are not included.

Military airfields

Photographs, maps and descriptions of RAF Stations within the UK during the Second World War can be found in AIR 10/4038 and 4039 as well as AIR 20/7585 and 7586. A selection of papers about the construction of airfields is in WORK 46/7-8. Information about the construction of airfields by the Royal Engineers in the UK and overseas is in WO 227/111. In addition, you may consult two ledgers in the Reference Room, entitled *Maps and Plans*, which include details of airfields. The two ledgers are a 'Summary Catalogue', which lists lettercodes and piece numbers, and a 'Subject Index', which lists subjects alphabetically.

Production of aircraft and supply of stores

In April 1939 the Cabinet approved the creation of a Ministry of Supply to provide stores which were in common use by the Army, Royal Navy and RAF. The Ministry of Aircraft Production was created in May 1940 to relieve the Air Ministry of responsibility for procurement of aircraft and associated supplies; the former Air Ministry department of the Air Member for Development and Production was transferred to this new Ministry. Matters relating to production and supply for the RAF can be found in the following:

AVIA 9   Ministry of Aircraft Production: Private Office Papers. This contains unregistered papers of Ministers and Parliamentary Secretaries, listed in date order, such as:
> 1940-1941 Aircraft and aircraft supplies for Australia
> 1941-1942 Expansion programme for Bomber Command ('The Clarion Call')
> 1942 Aircraft production programme
> 1942-1944 Jet propulsion and acquisition: Low attack aircraft by Power Jets Ltd.
> 1942-1945 Air Transport Auxiliary

AVIA 10   Ministry of Aircraft Production: Private Office Papers. This class has a key to headings for pieces 1-368 arranged alphabetically, such as:

> Air Supply Board
> Engines: research and development
> Radar and radio

The remaining pieces from 369 onwards are in numerical order under headings such as:

> Dam Busters Raid
> Cairncross, A K

AVIA 11   Ministry of Supply: Private Office Papers. This very small class includes some papers of the wartime Ministers and Parliamentary Secretaries.

AVIA 12   Ministry of Supply: Unregistered Papers. This consists mainly of records of the wartime Ministry of Supply, under headings arranged alphabetically, such as:

> Lend Lease
> Overseas Supplies
> Statistics

AVIA 15   Ministry of Aircraft Production Files. This is a very large class, indexed alphabetically under headings such as:

> Arms and Armament
> Contracts and Contractors
> Navigational Aids and Systems
> Purchases from abroad

AVIA 22   Ministry of Supply Registered Files. This is a very large class, with the piece numbers arranged in File Codes with headings that are not in any alphabetical order, such as:

> 213 Production Capacity
> 227 Publicity
> 237 Director of Scientific Research
> 274 Radio equipment and components
> 285 Explosives and chemical defence

AVIA 38   North American Supplies. This class contains material on the procurement of military supplies fron North America during the Second World War, in particular records of the British Purchasing Commission in the USA. It is arranged under alphabetical headings, such as:

> British Air Commission
> British Supply Council

Documents used in compiling Official Histories

Royal Aircraft Establishment

The Royal Aircraft Establishment (now the Defence Research Agency) at Farnborough is the country's chief centre for scientific research and experimental development. It is engaged in both theoretical and experimental work in the laboratory and in flight. Work carried out during the Second World War can be found in the following:

AVIA 6   Royal Aircraft Establishment Reports. This very large class contains reports arranged chronologically under headings such as:
> Aerodynamics
> Armament
> Electrical Engineering
> Engines
> Instruments
> Metallurgy
> Photography
> Radio

AVIA 13   Royal Aircraft Establishment, Registered Files. The pieces are arranged under headings such as:
> Engines
> Radio
> Aircraft Armament

Other establishments, committees and councils

Classes relating to research and development throughout the Second World War are as follows:

AIR 57   Director General of Medical Services. The RAF Flying Personnel Research Committee was formed in 1939 to advise the Secretary of State for Air on factors causing operational inefficiency in aircrew or impairing their chances of safety or survival. This class consists of a collection of the committee's reports and memoranda, with an index in pieces 24 to 26.

AIR 62   Whittle Papers. The papers relating to the development of the jet engine by Air Cdre Sir Frank Whittle and his company Power Jets

Ltd. This company was formed in 1936 and backed by the Air Ministry from the summer of 1939. Its work led to the production of the W1 jet engine and the first flight of the E28/39 Gloster aircraft on 15 May 1941. The pieces are arranged in date order and cover the period of the Second World War. They also include photographs.

AIR 64   Central Fighter Establishment. This was formed in October 1944 with the aim of increasing the effectiveness of fighter aircraft and the men who flew them. Examples of the pieces are:
> Air interception radar
> Employment of drop tanks as incendiary weapons
> Report on radio altimeter in Typhoon aircraft
> Gyro gun sight
> Trials of Loran radar in Mosquito aircraft

AIR 65   Air-Sea Development Unit Reports, such as:
> Anti-submarine equipment
> ASV (Air to surface vessel)
> Smoke markers

AVIA 7   Royal Radar Establishment Files. This establishment was named the Air Ministry Research Establishment (AMRE) in 1939 and renamed the Telecommunications Research Establishment (TRE) in 1940. It was responsible for scientific work associated with detection and location of aircraft. There is no index in this large class, but information and reports may be found under headings such as:
> Chain Home [radar stations]
> Eureka [radar beacon for glider operations]
> GCI [ground control interception]
> H2S [centrimentral navigation aid for aircraft]
> Loran [radio pulse system for long range navigation]
> Oboe [pulse type blind bombing device]
> Serrate [homing equipment and air interception to locate
>> enemy aircraft]

AVIA 16   Aircraft Torpedo Development Unit Reports. This unit, based at Gosport in Hampshire, was responsible for in-flight tests and development of torpedos, mines and pyrotechnics. The pieces concern tests made in combination with the Admiralty, in such aircraft as Beauforts, Hampdens, Beaufighters and Catalinas.

AVIA 18   Aeroplane and Armament Experimental Establishment: Reports and

Notes. Reports of this establishment, based at Boscombe Down in Wiltshire, are arranged under headings such as:
Aircraft Armament
Equipment
Instruments
Failures

AVIA 19   Marine Aircraft Experimental Establishment. Reports from this establishment, which moved from Felixstowe in Suffolk to Helensburgh in Scotland soon after the outbreak of war, can be found under headings such as:
Aircraft Armament Research
Engines
Instruments
Equipment
Operational Aircraft

AVIA 21   Airborne Forces Experimental Establishment. Reports from this establishment, which was formed at Ringway in Cheshire in mid-1940, moved to Elmet in Yorkshire in August 1942, and then to Beaulieu in Hampshire in January 1945, may be found on gliders, parachutes and towing aircraft.

AVIA 26   Royal Radar Establishment and predecessors. This contains reports, memoranda and technical notes in addition to those in AVIA 7 above.

AVIA 30   National Gas Turbine Establishment. This contains numerous Whittle drawings of combustion chambers and engines, etc.

AVIA 32   Aircraft Torpedo Development Unit. This contains pieces additional to those in AVIA 16 above.

AVIA 40   Rocket Propulsion Establishment. This contains technical reports on the initial development work carried out on rocket projectiles at the Government Projectile Establishment (PDE) at Aberforth in Cardiganshire during the Second World War.

AVIA 42   British Central Scientific Office: Registered Files. This contains reports on the office set up in Washington during March 1941 to continue the work of scientific co-operation between the USA and the UK.

Histories

Official histories form authoritative and useful general bases for research into any particular operations or spheres of RAF activity. They are to be found in the following:

AIR 41   Air Historical Branch: Narratives and Monographs. In the years following the cessation of hostilities, the AHB prepared numerous narratives and monographs in respect of the Second World War. These cover most of the conflicts in which the RAF was engaged. Examples, giving the dates they were completed, are:
>   1945 The Air Defence of Great Britain, Vol II: The Battle of Britain.
>   1947 The Liberation of North West Europe, Vol III: The Landings in Normandy.
>   1950 Signals, Vol IV: Radar in Raid Reporting.
>   1952 Air Defence of Great Britain, Vol VI: the Flying Bomb and Rocket Campaign, 1944 to 1945.
>   1958 RAF Operations in the Dodecanese Islands Sept-Nov 1943.

AIR 49   History of RAF Medical Services. The majority of the pieces in this class consist of records especially compiled for the Medical History of the War, covering not only the RAF but the other armed and civilian services. The pieces in this class are indexed under countries, Commands, Groups, Wings, Squadrons, Maintenance Units, Hospitals, Mobile Field Hospitals and Receiving Stations, Medical Field Consultants' Reports and Miscellaneous.

AVIA 46   Ministry of Supply Files: Series I (Establishment). This consists mainly of a historical series of files containing narratives and documents dealing with events before the Second World War. For instance, under 'Air Ministry' there are 'Type Biographies and Sources' of numerous aircraft such as:
>   1936-1945 AV Roe Lancaster
>   1942-1945 Mustang Aircraft
>   Under 'Narratives' there are:
>   1943 Aircraft programmes: quantities to 1943
>   1938-1945 Factories for repair of aircraft
>   1945 Reciprocating aero engines: design and development

Examples of research

Some practical examples of research carried out into the records of the RAF in the Second World War may assist you in identifying documents relevant to your own areas of interest.

A bombing operation

The fiftieth anniversary of the famous dam-busting operation by the Lancasters of 617 Squadron on the night of 16/17 May 1943 necessitated a listing of the records relating to this raid, for commemorative articles and a display board at the PRO. The planning, execution and effects of this raid were found in an exceptionally large number of documents, as follows:

AIR 2/4967 1943 Immediate awards: operational commands
AIR 4/37 1940 Nov-1944 Sept W/Cdr G P Gibson VC Pilot's Flying Log
          Book
AIR 6/63 1943 Jan-Dec Air Council Memoranda
AIR 6/67 1940 July-1943 Dec Conclusions of Air Council Meetings
AIR 8/1234 1943 Feb-1944 Mar Operations 'Upkeep' and 'Highball'
AIR 8/1237 1943 Mar-1944 Oct 'Highball' and 'Upkeep' progress reports
AIR 8/1238 1943 Mar-1944 Oct Destruction of German dams: economic
          effect
AIR 8/1239 1943 July-Aug Operation 'Chastise'. Russian request for
          information
AIR 8/1458 1943 Feb-1945 Mar Miscellaneous correspondence with Chief
          of Naval Staff
AIR 9/214 1941-1942 Joint Planning Staff: future strategy
AIR 9/215 1942-1943   "   "   "   "   "
AIR 9/216 1943   "   "   "   "   "
AIR 14/595 1943 Apr-Oct No. 617 Squadron: Operations against Dams
AIR 14/717 1943 Apr-1944 Oct 617 and 619 Squadrons: operations
AIR 14/790 1942 June-1945 Apr Operational research Committee
AIR 14/817 1940 July-1941 June Attacks on German reservoirs and dams
AIR 14/840 1943 Feb-June Operation 'Chastise' (with photographs)
AIR 14/842 1943 Mar-May 'Upkeep': Progress reports
AIR 14/844 1943 May Operation 'Chastise'
AIR 14/1195 1941 18 Dec-1943 19 July Bomber Command operations
AIR 14/2036 1943 May Operation 'Chastise'
AIR 14/2060 1943 July-1944 Dec Further trials with 'Upkeep'
AIR 14/2061 1943 Mar-1945 Apr   "   "   "
AIR 14/2062 1943 Apr Operational role of No 617 Squadron

AIR 14/2087 1943 May-June Operation 'Chastise'

AIR 14/2088 1943 May Operation 'Chastise'

AIR 14/2144 1942 Nov-1943 Oct Intelligence Watch Diary No 5 Group Vol VI

AIR 19/305 1941-1943 Publicity in USA.

AIR 19/383 Attack on the Ruhr dams and the defence of UK dams and reservoirs (with photographs)

AIR 20/2617 1943 Mar-1944 July Operations 'Highball' and 'Upkeep', reports and papers

AIR 22/129 1943 Apr-May Air Ministry War Room Sumary

AIR 24/205 1943 Jan-Dec Bomber Command Operations Record Book

AIR 24/254 1943 Apr 1 Bomber Command Appendixes

AIR 24/255 1943 May   "   "   "

AIR 25/119 1943 Feb-June No 5 (Bomber) Group Operations Record Book

AIR 27/2128 1943 Apr-1945 May No 617 Squadron Operations Record Book

AIR 27/2130 1943 Apr-1945 Dec No 618 Squadron Operations Record Book

AIR 28/683 1943 Jan-1945 Dec RAF Scampton Operations Record Book

AIR 28/690 1943 Jan-June RAF Scampton Appendixes

AIR 34/609 1943 Feb-1945 Jan Moehne and Eder Dams: interpretation reports and photographs

AVIA 10/369 1942 Result Book (manuscript and photograph) of tests at Nant-y-Gro dam and on models in connection with 'Dam Busting Raid' 1943: Vol II

AVIA 10/370 1942-1943 'Dam Busting Raid': Vol III

    [MFQ 633] 1943 German drawings of breach in Moehne Dam

    [MFQ 634] 1944 German drawing of defence errected in Moehne Dam after this attack

AVIA 18/715 1941-1951 Aeroplane and Armament Experimental Establishment: Lancaster performance and handling trials [includes modified Lancaster III serial ED 825/G, with photographs]

CAB 65/34 1943 Apr 1-June 29 War Cabinet minutes, conclusions

CAB 65/37 1943 Jan 11-Mar 29 War Cabinet minutes, confidential annexes

CAB 65/38 1943 Apr 5-June 3 War Cabinet minutes, confidential annexes

CAB 66/36 1943 War Cabinet memoranda

CAB 66/37 1943   "   "   "

CAB 69/5 1943 Feb 23-Dec 12 War Cabinet Defence Comittee (Operations), Minutes of Meetings and Papers

CAB 79/26 1943 Feb 26-Apr 12. War Cabinet Chiefs of Staff Committee minutes

CAB 79/27 1943 Apr 15-Nov 11. War Cabinet Chiefs of Staff Committee minutes

CAB 80/39 1943 Jan 13-Mar 27 War Cabinet Chiefs of Staff Committee Memoranda

The life of an aircraft

In 1991 the Court of the Crown Prince of Bahrain required a short history to be written about a Spitfire Mark VB serial W3632, which was financed by the residents of Bahrain and taken on charge by the RAF on 21 July 1941, remaining in service until struck off charge on 29 November 1945. Using as a guide a transcript of the Aircraft Record Card, Air Ministry Form 78, held by the AHB, the following records were researched to compile the history:

AIR 27/512 Jan 1941-Dec 1941 54 Squadron Operations Record Book
AIR 27/919 May 1941-Dec 1943 124   "   "   "   "
AIR 27/1728 Jan 1942-Dec 1943 332   "   "   "   "
AIR 27/1737 Nov 1931-Nov 1945 340 "   "   "   "
AIR 27/1738 Jan 1943-Nov 1944 341   "   "   "   "
AIR 27/1933 Apr 1941-June 1945 485 "   "   "   "
AIR 27/2079 Sept 1925-Dec 1943 603 "   "   "   "
AIR 28/384 Oct 1915-Dec 1941 Hornchurch "   "   "
AIR 28/512 Jan 1916-Dec 1941 Manston   "   "   "
AIR 29/682 Mar 1941-Apr 1947 54 OTU   "   "   "
AIR 29/683 June 1940-May 1945 57 OTU   "   "   "
AIR 29/963 Oct 1938-Dec 1945 6 MU   "   "   "
AIR 29/967 Mar 1939-Dec 1945 9 MU   "   "   "
AIR 29/991 Oct 1940-Dec 1945 29 MU   "   "   "
AIR 50/21 Feb 1940-Nov 1945 54 Squadron Combat Reports
AIR 50/167 Oct 1939-Feb 1942 603   "   "   "

In addition, by consulting the RAF Retired List and *Who's Who*, the pilot who flew the Spitfire on the majority of its operations, which were in 54 and 603 Squadrons, was located; he was able to add many accurate and personal details to the history.

A Roll of Honour

In 1989, RAF St Mawgan in Cornwall requested the compilation of a Book of Remembrance to commemorate all those who died either when flying from nearby RAF St Eval or at this Station during the Second World War. St Eval was a Coastal Command Station which opened on 2 October 1939 and closed on 6 March 1959, and during that period the St Eval Parish Church was situated within its perimeter track.

Many Squadrons or detachments of Squadrons came to St Ival and then departed during the Second World War, and the first task for the researchers was

to establish the critreria for entry of names into the Book of Remembrance.
It was decided that it should include all those:

(1) who were killed on the Station, either accidentally or as a result of enemy bombing, and

(2) who were killed when flying from Squadrons based at the Station or in detachment there, even though the aircraft might have touched down on other Stations before continuing their operations.

Those who were killed when flying from other Stations but who touched down at St Eval while en route to their targets were not included, nor were those from Squadrons based at St Eval but on detachment at other Stations.
The following records were examined first:

AIR 28/729 Nov 1939-Dec 1942 St Eval Operations Record Book
AIR 28/730 Jan 1943-Dec 1944   "   "   "   "
AIR 28/731 Jan-Dec 1945   "   "   "   "
AIR 28/732 Nov 1939-Dec 1940 St Eval Appendixes
AIR 28/733 Jan 1940-Nov 1942   "   "
AIR 28/734 Jan-Apr 1941   "   "
AIR 28/735 May-July 1941   "   "
AIR 28/736 Aug-Oct 1941   "   "
AIR 28/737 Nov 1941-Feb 1942   "   "
AIR 28/738 Mar-July 1942   "   "
AIR 28/739 Aug-Oct 1942   "   "
AIR 28/740 Nov 1942-Apr 1943   "   "
AIR 28/741 Jan 1943-Aug 1944   "   "
AIR 28/742 May-Aug 1943   "   "
AIR 28/743 Sept-Oct 1943   "   "
AIR 28/744 Nov-Dec 1943   "   "
AIR 28/745 Jan-Feb 1944   "   "
AIR 28/746 Mar-Apr 1944   "   "
AIR 28/747 May-June 1944   "   "
AIR 28/748 July-Aug 1944   "   "
AIR 28/749 Sept-Oct 1944   "   "
AIR 28/750 Nov-Dec 1944   "   "
AIR 28/751 Jan-Feb 1945   "   "
AIR 28/752 Mar-May 1945   "   "

From these records numerous names of those known to have lost their lives or to have failed to return from operations were listed. These names were checked in the following records and more names were discovered:

AIR 27/278 Aug 1915-Dec 1941 22 Squadron Operations Record Book
AIR 27/279 Jan 1942-June 1946 22 Squadron   "   "   "
AIR 27/504 Jan-Dec 1941 53 Squadron   "   "   "
AIR 27/505 Jan 1942-Dec 1943 53 Squadron   "   "   "
AIR 27/506 Jan-Dec 1944 53 Squadron   "   "   "
AIR 27/544 Jan 1941-Dec 1943 58 Squadron   "   "   "
AIR 27/682 Jan 1942-June 1943 82 Squadron   "   "   "
AIR 27/708 Dec 1940-Dec 1943 86 Squadron   "   "   "
AIR 27/801 Mar 1928-Dec 1941 101 Squadron   "   "   "
AIR 27/978 June 1941-Dec 1943 143 Squadron   "   "   "
AIR 27/1128 Jan 1944-Sept 1946 179 Squadron   "   "   "
AIR 27/1223 Jan 1941-Dec 1943 206 Squadron   "   "   "
AIR 27/1338 Oct 1914-May 1940 217 Squadron   "   "   "
AIR 27/1339 Oct 1939-July 1940 217 Squadron   "   "   "
AIR 27/1340 June-Dec 1940 217 Squadron   "   "   "
AIR 27/1341 Jan 1941-Sept 1945 217 Squadron   "   "   "
AIR 27/1366 Jan 1941-Dec 1943 220 Squadron   "   "   "
AIR 27/1368 Nov 1940-Dec 1943 221 Squadron   "   "   "
AIR 27/1386 Jan-Dec 1941 224 Squadron   "   "   "
AIR 27/1387 Jan-Dec 1942 224 Squadron   "   "   "
AIR 27/1388 Jan-Dec 1943 224 Squadron   "   "   "
AIR 27/1389 Jan 1944-June 1945 224 Squadron   "   "   "
AIR 27/1431 Jan 1941-Dec 1942 233 Squadron   "   "   "
AIR 27/1439 Oct 1939-Dec 1943 234 Squadron   "   "   "
AIR 27/1445 Oct 1939-Dec 1940 236 Squadron   "   "   "
AIR 27/1446 Jan-Dec 1941 236 Squadron   "   "   "
AIR 27/1447 Jan-Dec 1942 236 Squadron   "   "   "
AIR 27/1487 Nov 1939-Dec 1941 247 Squadron   "   "   "
AIR 27/1609 Nov 1941-Dec 1943 279 Squadron   "   "   "
AIR 27/1786 May 1941-May 1945 404 Squadron   "   "   "
AIR 27/1794 Jan 1943-Dec 1944 407 Squadron   "   "   "
AIR 27/1818 Dec 1941-June 1945 417 Squadron   "   "   "
AIR 27/1959 Jan 1942-Dec 1943 502 Squadron   "   "   "
AIR 27/1984 Sept 1943-May 1945 517 Squadron   "   "   "
AIR 27/2025 Oct 1942-Oct 1943 543 Squadron   "   "   "
AIR 27/2033 Oct 1942-July 1944 547 Squadron   "   "   "
AIR 27/2034 Aug 1944-July 1945 547 Squadron   "   "   "
AIR 27/2113 Jan-Dec 1941 612 Squadron   "   "   "
AIR 27/2114 Jan-Dec 1942 612 Squadron   "   "   "
AIR 29/414 Jan-Dec 1941 1 PRU   "   "   "
AIR 29/415 Jan-Oct 1942 1 PRU   "   "   "
AIR 29/638 1940 Apr-1943 Dec 10 OTU   "   "   "

Since these records seldom contained positive news of the fates of those who failed to return, the following was then examined:

AIR 20/2336 1945 Mar British, Dominion and Allied PoWs in Germany and
          German-occupied territories

Some names were eliminated from this record. Next, the ledger *RAF War Dead 1939-48* at St Catherine's House in London was consulted. This gives the names, ranks, service numbers and units of RAF airmen and airwomen who were killed outside the shores of the United Kingdom. However, it does not include those from Dominion Air Forces. These names were checked in the ledgers at the RAF Church of St Clement Dane's in Aldwych. Although these ledgers do not give ranks or unit numbers, researchers were able to verify some names which were easily distinguishable.

Apart from these researches in public records, parishioners at St Eval examined local police records, since the police were advised of airmen who failed to return from operations in case the aircraft were found to have crashed in the locality.

Following these researches, there remained a large number of queries. It was therefore necessary for serving officers at RAF St Mawgan to make a series of visits to the AHB, to examine personal records which are not available to civilian researchers and ascertain what had happened to the airmen. Some names were found to have been misspelt in the Squadron records, while other men had been picked up from dinghies.

In addition, a few aircraft of the USAAF and the USNAF were lost from this Station, and it was necessary to seek the help of a specialist researcher who corresponded with official bodies in the USA and verified the fates of the airmen.

In all, the fates of over 2000 airmen were examined, the research being spread over a period of about two years. The resulting Book of Remembrance, prepared and illuminated by a local artist, was dedicated at St Eval Parish Church on 20 September 1992. It contains 823 names, but the researchers cannot be absolutely sure that all have been discovered since, if they had been omitted from the records consulted, it was not possible to identify them.

figure 15: German invasion barges at Dunkirk, 1940 (AIR 34/741)

A concentration of German invasion barges assembled at Dunkirk, photographed on 19 September 1940 from 3,100 feet by Blenheim IV serial T2032 of 82 Squadron, flown by Plt Off Metcalfe. Twelve Blenheims took off from Bodney in Norfolk for bombing and photo-reconnaissance sorties over the port. Eleven turned back since there was no cloud cover but Metcalfe continued alone and carried out the attack, returning with his aircraft holed by flak.

figure 16: German base Herdla under attack, 1941 (AIR 34/745)

On 27 December 1941, thirteen Blenheim IVs of 114 Squadron from West Raynham in Norfolk raided the German fighter base at Herdla, near Bergen, as part of a diversion when British Commandos landed at Vaagsö. No Blenheims were lost from enemy action but two collided and crashed. This photograph shows bombs bursting and machine-gun fire in the water.

figure 17: Ford Truck factory, Poissy (near Paris), under attack, 1942 (AIR 34/745)

On 8 March 1942, twelve Douglas Boston IIIs of 88 and 226 Squadrons, part of Bomber Command's 2 Group, made a low-level attack on the Ford Truck factory at Poissy (near Paris), causing considerable damage. One Boston was lost.

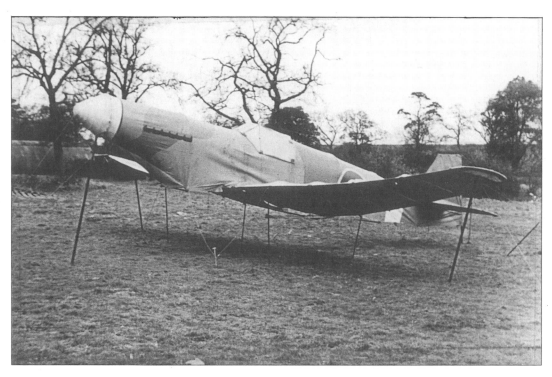

figure 18: Dummy Spitfire and Mustang aircraft (AIR 20/4349)

A mobile dummy Spitfire (top) and a mobile dummy Mustang (bottom), two of many erected on dummy airfields to deceive unwary airmen of the Luftwaffe.

R.A.F. Form 540

See instructions on use of this form in K.R. and A.C.I., para 2349 and War Manual Pt. II, chapter XX. and also in R.A.F. Pocket Book.

OPERATIONS RECORD BOOK

STATION
of (Unit or Formation) / HEADQUARTERS R.A.F. SCAMPTON.

No. of pages used for day:

Page No. 3

SECRET.

Place	Date	Time	Summary of Events	References to Appendices
	15th May.		AERODROME SERVICEABILITY: - No change. No Operations.	
	16th May.		No. 617 SQUADRON OPERATED FROM SCAMPTON FOR THE FIRST TIME WITH 19 LANCASTERS.	
			No. 617 SQUADRON was formed on the 24th March 1943, and after six weeks training	
			were detailed on the evening of the 16th May to attack the German dams.	
			3 Lancasters were unsuccessful and returned for various reasons.	
			8 returned having successfully completed their task.	
			8 are missing of which 3 are known to have delivered attacks on their targets.	
			As a result of this raid the Mohne and Eder Dams were breached and the structure of the	
			Sorpe Dam seriously damaged.	
			The attack was led by Wing Commander G.P. GIBSON, D.S.O. and Bar, D.F.C. and Bar, who	
			was awarded the Victoria Cross.	
	17th May.		AERODROME SERVICEABILITY: - No change.	
			No operations by 5 Group tonight.	
	18th May.		AERODROME SERVICEABILITY: - No change.	
			No operations tonight.	
	19th May.		AERODROME SERVICEABILITY: - No change.	
			No operations tonight.	
	20th May.		AERODROME SERVICEABILITY: - / No change. No operations in No. 5 Group tonight.	
	21st May.		AERODROME SERVICEABILITY: - No change.	
			Bomber Command stand down tonight.	
	22nd May.		AERODROME SERVICEABILITY: - No change.	
			Bomber Command stand down tonight.	
	23rd May.		AERODROME SERVICEABILITY: - No change.	
			BOMBING OPERATIONS ON DORTMUND. NIGHT 23rd/24th May, 1943.	
			24 Lancasters of No. 57 Squadron took off to carry out the above operation. One	
			Lancaster returned to base with intercomm. u/s, and 2 failed to return. 21 Lancasters	
			landed safely at Scampton upon completion of the operation.	
	24th May.		AERODROME SERVICEABILITY: - No change. BOMBER COMMAND STAND DOWN.	

figure 19: Operations Record Book for RAF Scampton, 15-16 May 1943: Dambusters raid (AIR 28/682)

The Operations Record Book of RAF Scampton, the station from which 617 Squadron flew on 16/17 May 1943, on the famous dam-busting raid.

Compiled by S/LDR. T.H.W. PEARCE.

OPERATIONS RECORD BOOK

of (Unit or Formation) R.A.F. TARRANT RUSHTON.

Page No........

No. of pages used for day........

SECRET.

R.A.F. Form 540
See instructions for use of this form in K.R. and A.C.I., para. 2349, and War Manual Pt. II, chapter XX, and notes in R.A.F. Pocket Book.

Place	Date	Time	Summary of Events	References to Appendices
	1944. June 1		**OPERATIONS.** Cloudy with drizzle during morning becoming fair towards dusk.	
	2		**Fair.** Good visibility.	
	3		As 2nd/but cloud generally more.	
	4	20.00	Film of area of forthcoming operations was shown to all aircrew and glider pilots in the Briefing Room and again an hour later.	
	5		Fair to cloudy with rain in evening. Operations "COUP DE MAIN". Intention to land 174 troops to capture in tact bridges across Caen Canal and River Orne N. of Caen. 6 Halifax/Horsa combinations were used and to disguise their intention were to drop 12 500 M.B. instantaneous bombs on Powder Factory situated S.E. of CAEN after releasing gliders. All aircraft returned to base. 5 aircraft bombed the target but one failed to locate it. Operation "TONGA". 30 Halifax V aircraft detailed to release Horsa Gliders alongside L.Z. 'N' East of CAEN Canal and drop 9 containers per aircraft on a D.Z. to the south of the L.Z. 4 Halifax V aircraft detailed to release Hamilcar Gliders loaded with 17 pounder guns over L.Z. 'N'. One aircraft K.288 (Pilot F/O ANDERSON) failed to return from this operation whilst 5 aircraft failed to release gliders over the L.Z.	
	6		Cloudy with slight showers in evening. Operation "MALLARD". 30 Halifax V detailed to release Hamilcar gliders over L.Z. 'N'. 2 Halifax V detailed to release Horsa gliders over L.Z. 'N' and drop 18 containers on D.Z. (68766 Sheet 7 F.2 1/50.000). One aircraft (Pilot P/O CARPENTER) failed to return from this operation.	
	7		Fair to cloudy. DAKOTA 326 'V' of No. 62 Troop Carrier Squadron. Station SALTBY, landed on return from supply dropping mission over CHERBOURG PENINSULA. Starboard engine oil tank shot up.	
	8./		Cloudy with slight rain about dawn.	

figure 20: Operations Record Book for Tarrant Ruston: first aircraft to take off for D-day, June 1944 (AIR 28/818)

Part of the Operations Record Book of RAF Tarrant Ruston in Dorset for the night of 5/6 June 1944, showing the towing by Halifaxes of six Horsa gliders to release points near bridges over the river Orne and the Caen Canal, which were then captured by airborne troops a few hours before the D-day landings on the coast of Normandy and enabled the British Second Army to advance from its bridgehead.

figure 21: Operations Record Book for RAF Langham, 15 June 1944: D-day
(AIR 28/444)

On 15 June 1944, Coastal Command's Strike Wings at Langham in Norfolk and
North Coates in Lincolnshire combined to attack a German convoy which had
left Rotterdam for the Baltic, as shown in this Operations Record Book of
Langham. Forty-two Beaufighters took off from the two stations, escorted by ten
Mustangs from Coltishall in Norfolk. They sank the two main ships in the
convoy, *Nachtigall* of 3,500 tons and *Amerskerk* of 7.900 tons. They also sank one
of the seven escorting minesweepers and damaged all the others. No aircraft
were lost, although several were hit by flak.

OPERATIONS RECORD BOOK

of (Unit or Formation) ROYAL AIR FORCE STATION, LANGHAM.

SECRET.

R.A.F. Form 540

Place	Date	Time	Summary of Events	References to Appendices
LANGHAM.	13.6.44.	20.30	**Operations (Contd.)** Six Aircraft of 489 Squadron did an anti E. Boat patrol from BARFLEUR to CAP DE LA HAGUE without result.	
	14.6.44.		**Personnel.** W/O. E. M. KAY (Ops. Room) posted out to S/Ldr. F. D. HOLMES (Accts) posted in. **Weather.** Wind W. 5 - 10 m.p.h. becoming 15 - 20 m.p.h. in late morning. Mainly fair.	
		03.32.	Cloud 2/3,000 ft. Very good visibility. **Operations.** Six Aircraft each from 455 and 489 Squadrons did an anti E. Boat patrol from NORTH COATES. Attacks were made on small minesweepers, but no results observed.	
			Administration. The New Zealand Prime Minister, Mr. Fraser, and Mrs. Fraser visited the station and mer carried personnel of No. 489 Squadron. They stayed to lunch and left at 14.30 hours.	
	15.6.44.	05.00	**Weather.** Wind W. 5 - 10 m.p.h. Cloud 2/3,000 ft. Visibility - good. Weather fair. **Operations.** Thirty Beaufighters Anti-Flak and ten Torbeaus made rendezvous at SOUTHWALD AHEAD. The force was composed of LANGHAM and NORTH COATES Wings, led by Wing Commander GADD. Very good results were achieved without loss to our Aircraft. A W/V of 8,000 tons and a large naval auxiliary were sunk. At least four escorts sunk and the remainder badly damaged and set on fire. Congratulatory messages were received from A.O.C. in C., A.O.C. No. 16 Group and 2nd T.A.C. MORE.	
			Administration. 2420 R.A.F. Regiment Squadron reversed to state "E" manning at first light. **Personnel.** W/O. J. W. CUTHBRIDGE (Signals) posted out. F/Lt. B. A. BUTLER (Tech. I.O.) ceased temporary duty and returned to BIRCHAM NEWTON.	
	16.6.44.	23.15	**Weather.** Wind W. 10 - 15 m.p.h. Veering N. before midnight. Cloudy with slight rain. in the afternoon. Cloud base 1/2,000 ft. Vis. good at first becoming 4 - 6 miles. **Operations.** At five minute intervals from time stated, three pairs of Beaufighters of 455 Squadron carried out anti E. Boat patrols from GRAVELINES TO OSTEND. Probable damage to two or more E. Boats claimed.	
	17.6.44.	22.00	**Weather.** Wind N. 20-25 m.p.h. Gusty, veering to N.W. before midnight. Cloudy. Cloud base 1500-2000 ft. Vis. 10-20 miles falling to 8 miles late in period. **Operations.** Two Aircraft of 489 Squadron carried out a recce. into the HELIGOLAND BIGHT without result.	
	18.6.44.	04.30	**Operations.** 12 Beaus. with 12 from NORTH COATES carried out anti-E-boat patrol from GRAVELINES to THE HOOK, led by S/L. MONNUIAN of 489 Sqn. Two "M" M/S were seriously damaged, with one hit. Two Beaus of 489 (G/L. MONNIHAM and F/O. BOLLARD) failed to return. **Weather.** Wind N-NE 10-15 mph. Cloudy, cloud base 1500' at first lifting to 3000' by midday, falling to 1000-1500' in evening. Vis. 8-15 miles.	
	19.6.44.	0500	No operations. **Weather.** Wind N-NW 10-15 mph. Cloudy, fine in evening. Cloud base 6-800', dispersing late afternoon. Vis. 4-6 miles. **Operations.** 6 Beaus. of 489 Sqn. with torps. 6 with cannon and 12 of 455 Sqn. with cannon, together with 6 T.F. Beaus. of 236 Sqn. from North Coates and escorted by a Sqn. of Mustangs from SOUTHWALD did an armed sweep along the Dutch coast. The force was led by W/Cdr. GADD. Wing of 455 Sqn. No sighting was made.	
	20.6.44.	1228	**Weather.** Wind NE 15-20 mph. Gusty. Cloudy with drizzle. Cloud base 4-600'. Vis. 4-6 miles. **Operations.** 1 Beau. of 455 Sqn. did a special recce. from THE HOOK to DEN HELDER without result.	
		1600	2 Beaus. of 455 Sqn. did recce. in the HELIGOLAND BIGHT without result. **Personnel.** W/O. A. W. HINDS. (operroom) posted to MIDENHY ISLAND. W/O. J. W. MONTGOMERY (ops room) posted from H.Q. 16 Group. W.A. PARKER (Australian War Correspondent) visited the station.	
	21.6.44.		**Weather.** Weather cloudy with drizzle in morning. Wind NNE 15 mph. Vis. 1 - 6 miles. No operations. **Personnel.** W. W. HOOPER (War Correspondent) paid a one-day visit.	

figure 22: 1st Dorsets landing on D-day, 1944 (AIR 40/1959, p 92)

The 1st Dorsets landing between Le Hamel and Les Roquettes on Jig Beach, part of the Gold Area, on D-day, 6 June 1944. Together with the 1st Hampshires on their right, they formed the 231st Brigade of XXX Corps. Preceded by flail tanks and armoured vehicles of the Royal Engineers, the 1st Dorsets captured all their objectives.

figure 23: Mulberry harbour, 1944 (AIR 37/1231, p 51)

The Mulberry artificial harbour at Arromanches in the British Gold area, photographed on 2 October 1944. Another artificial harbour was constructed further west, off St Laurent in the American Omaha area. They consisted of blockships with pre-fabricated concrete caissons which formed breakwaters, as well as pier units. The two harbours were almost completed by mid-June 1944 before a great gale blew up from the north-east. This photograph was taken after reconstruction.

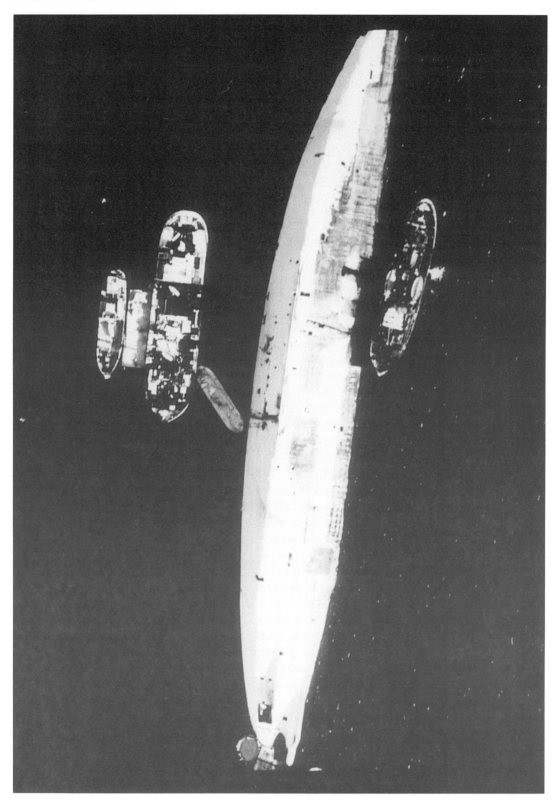

figure 24: Tirpitz at Tromsö, 1945 (AIR 34/100)

The capsized hull of the battleship *Tirpitz* at Tromsö, photographed on 22 March 1945, after being hit on 12 November 1944 by 12,000lb bombs dropped by Lancasters of 9 and 617 Squadrons operating from Lossiemouth. Snow covers much of the hull, but a hole can be identified on the starboard side between X and Y turrets, while four salvage vessels lie alongside the wreck. This oblique photograph was taken from 2,500 feet by Mosquito PR XVI serial NS637 of 544 Squadron from Benson, crewed by Sqn Ldr F L Dodd, DSO, AFC, and Plt Off E Hill, DFM. According to the squadron records they flew through intense flak to 'renew aquaintance' with the battleship.

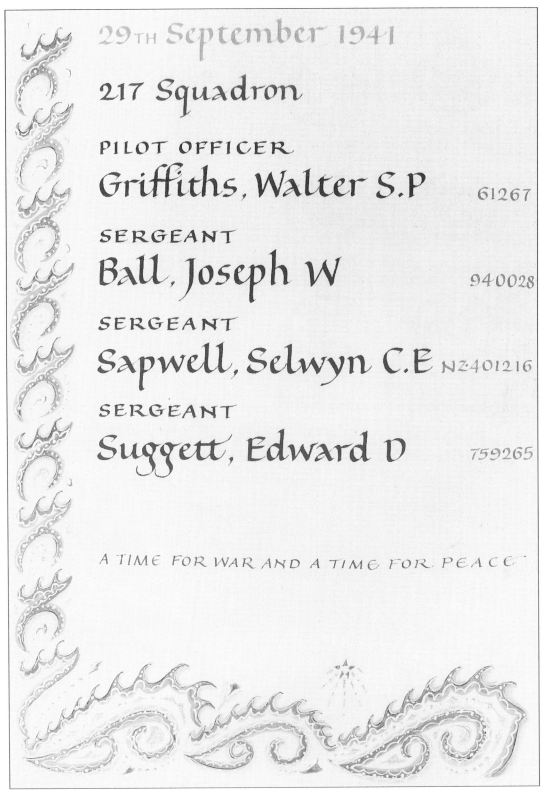

29TH September 1941

217 Squadron

PILOT OFFICER
Griffiths, Walter S.P   61267

SERGEANT
Ball, Joseph W   940028

SERGEANT
Sapwell, Selwyn C.E NZ401216

SERGEANT
Suggett, Edward D   759265

A TIME FOR WAR AND A TIME FOR PEACE

figure 25: St Eval Church: page from the Book of Remembrance, 1992
The Parish Church of St Eval was originally built in Norman times and stood within the RAF airfield from its opening on 2 October 1939 to its closure on 6 March 1959. It was refurbished as an RAF Church by the local parishioners and dedicated at a service on 1 October 1989. The Book of Remembrance was worked by Mrs Wendy Selby of Newquay, a Fellow of the Society of Scribes and Illuminators, and dedicated at the Battle of Britain Service on 20 September 1992. The photograph shows a page from the Book, in which are inscribed over 800 names.

Master Aircrew

Aircrew 1

Aircrew 2   Aircrew 3

Aircrew 4   Aircrew Cadet

aircrew NCO badges 1946-1950

Air Quartermaster   Air Electronics Operator

Air Load Master   Fighter Controller

post-war flying badges

Air Steward's badge

Post-war service badges

SECTION FOUR
Post-War RAF Sources
by
Christina Goulter

After the end of the Second World War, the RAF was not permitted to rest for long. Two forces threatened to destabilize the post-war world order: anti-colonialism and the spread of Communism. Reaction to these meant that British armed forces were engaged in a series of limited wars and counter-insurgency operations around the globe over a twenty-five year period. The brunt of the fighting was borne by the Army, but the RAF made essential contributions in tactical support and transport roles.

Apart from these world-wide operations, the RAF's post-war history, until the 1960s, was dominated by its responsibility for maintaining Britain's strategic nuclear deterrent. The British government's decision in January 1947 to develop the atomic weapon, coupled with the on-going predominance of strategic bombing doctrine in Air Ministry thinking, led to the establishment of the V-Force of Bomber Command, so-called because of the three aircraft which were to designed to deliver the atomic weapon: the Valiant, Victor and Vulcan.

The decision to adopt a nuclear strategy was spurred by the Cold War, and one of the first tangible expressions of the divide between the former wartime Western Allies and the Soviet Union was the blockading of Berlin by the Soviets in 1948. The air supply operation which ensued proved to be one of the RAF's greatest achievements.

Each of the principal post-war operations is dealt with in turn below, as are other important features of the post-war period, including the demobilization of the RAF, its role in the occupation of Germany after May 1945, and the restructuring of the defence body, responding both to cuts in defence expenditure and Great Britain's commitment to the North Atlantic Treaty Organization (NATO).

Unfortunately for the researcher, the RAF's post-war history is far less well signposted by official histories and 'in house' narratives compared with the First and Second World Wars and the inter-war period. However, in areas where such texts do exist, titles are listed alongside PRO references, and you are strongly advised to consult them before moving on to the primary records. Under the Public Records Acts 1958 and 1967, governmental records are made available to the public after a term of thirty years. Therefore only those RAF records up to 1963 are dealt with in this Guide. In cases where RAF operations span either side of 1963, or where records are close to being released, or a limited selection has been released, as in the case of documents relating to the Indonesian 'Confrontation' of 1963-1966, some reference is made to these operations. In places where it is felt that PRO sources can be augmented by other archival collections, the relevant institutions are listed. One of the problems associated with researching the RAF's post-war history is the relative paucity of documentation, compared with the Second World War. The momentous events of the war years tended to overshadow any subsequent developments. One such area is Search and Rescue.[1]

Demobilization

The immediate task facing the RAF in 1945 was its return to peacetime functioning. At home, the RAF had to demobilize its force of over 1,000,000 personnel, and cut down its equipment and facilities which, at the end of hostilities, amounted to 9,204 aircraft in 460 squadrons, and some 1,200 airfields. The process was carried out for the most part successfully, so that by April 1947 the RAF's strength was under 300,000 men and women, and 1,363 aircraft in 141 squadrons. Most of the aircraft struck off charge went to fuel a metal hungry industry, but a sizeable proportion went to overseas air forces.

Much of the important documentation concerning demobilization comprises files which were opened in 1944. However, the files which remain refer largely to demobilization in the overseas Commands, in AIR 23. This can be explained by the fact that difficulties in implementing demobilization and repatriation from some of the overseas Commands led to a number of disturbances in 1945 and 1946, including a 'strike' by airmen at RAF Seletar in Singapore and similar action at RAF Drigh Road and RAF Dum Dum in India. There was strong feeling among those serving overseas that their compatriots at home were pouring out of the RAF (and the other Services), and were taking the most attractive civilian jobs. There was also an uneasy feeling that the Army and the Navy were being given priority in demobilization. There was an element of truth in this latter conviction. Heavy losses of Allied shipping during the war meant that there was a heavy dependence upon air transport for the repatriation of Servicemen, and the staffing of the bases along air routes had to be done by RAF personnel. There was another aspect. The minute hostilities were over, various national airlines competed with each other over routes, and RAF presence in the Middle and Far East was seen as a means of staking British claims.

A 'grass roots' view of demobilization can be obtained from squadron and unit diaries in AIR 27 and station records in AIR 28. In between Service post and release into civilian life, an individual had first to go through what was known as a Personnel Despatch Centre, and records dealing with the immediate post-war period (1945-1947) can be found in AIR 29/1098-1100. If you are interested in the repatriation of Commonwealth (particularly Australian and New Zealand) airmen and officers, you should consult AIR 29/1099. This deals with

[1] Among the few files remaining are AIR 20/7003 and AIR 20/7151, both policy documents from the 1950s.

No 11 Personnel Reception and Despatch Centre at Brighton. Other later documents include AIR 29/2381, No 5 Personnel Despatch Unit (1951-1955).

A more general view of the problems associated with demobilization can be found in documents such as AIR 20/9244 Incidents at RAF stations in South-East Asia Command (1945-1946), AIR 23/1986 Brief history of events associated with the disaffection and 'strikes' among RAF units of ACSEA, AIR 20/9244 Incidents at RAF stations in South-East Asia Command (1945-1946), and AIR 23/2363 Operation of the release scheme (1946). Some of the files concerning the strikes are closed to public view until 1996, including AIR 20/9245 Strikes in South-East Asia Command (1945-1946). Policy records can be found in files such as AIR 23/1163-1164 Post-war release and demobilization - organizational policy (1944-1946), and AIR 23/2321-2322 Demobilization and Release Scheme - policy (1946).

The disposal of aircraft after the war is a subject dealt with in a number of AIR classes. Most of the aircraft which were not scrapped were exported. A large proportion of the American aircraft supplied to the RAF under the Lend/Lease programme were returned to the USA, including Mustangs, Bostons and Mitchells. Other Second World War vintage aircraft went on to serve with distinction with other air forces in later conflicts, most notably the use made by the French Air Force of ex-RAF Mosquitoes and Spitfires in Indochina during the late 1940s. The best collection of documents concerning exports of aircraft to overseas air forces is to be found in AIR 20, Code 5/25; for example, AIR 20/7447 Aircraft for France: policy (1950-1952). One important document which will appear in this series shortly is Exports of Military Aircraft. This piece gives a breakdown by aircraft type of all exports between 1945 and 1965.

RAF Germany, the Berlin Airlift 1948-1949, NATO, and nuclear deterrence

At the conclusion of the Second World War, Germany was to have been divided into four Zones of Occupation, under American, French, British and Soviet control. In effect, only two zones emerged, one under the control of the Western Allies, and the second an Eastern Zone under Soviet control. Within the Western Zone, the RAF's 2nd Tactical Air Force (TAF), which had fought its way across Europe, was replaced in July 1945 by a new organization, British Air Forces of Occupation (BAFO), a title deliberately chosen. Foremost among its roles was support of the British land forces in their task of occupation. BAFO was also responsible for the disbandment of the Luftwaffe and the disposal of its aircraft.

Considering the importance of BAFO, it is surprising that an official narrative history does not, as yet, exist. One is under way, but it will be some time before this is released for public view. In the meantime, you need to make a direct approach to the documents. BAFO has been devoted a whole PRO class, AIR 55, and this covers all aspects of operations, administration, and disarmament, and includes Orders of Battle for 2nd TAF. BAFO headquarters material is also found in AIR 24 Commands, in AIR 24/1804-1867. Additional information on the establishment of BAFO can be found in AIR 8 and AIR 20. The following is a selection of documents which provide a useful introduction to the subject:

> AIR 8/1125 Post-war control in Germany - higher appointments (Mar-Nov 1945)
> AIR 8/1434 Organization of RAF HQs (Oct 1945-Feb 1950)
> AIR 20/6475 TAF: Post-war organization to meet Occupation require ments (1943-1948)
> AIR 20/6898 BAFO Chain of Command (1946-1948)
> AIR 20/6963 BAFO Operational and Administrative role (1948-1951)

BAFO's own 'Command' record is to be found in AIR 24. Items 686-702 cover the months July to December 1945, and 1804-1867 the years 1946 to 1950. As with the subject of demobilization, you need sometimes to step back into war-time files, and this is the case particularly when dealing with the policy for the surrender and disposal of German aircraft. See especially the following:

> AIR 8/1159 German Aircraft: policy for surrender and disposal (May-July 1944)
> AIR 8/1127 Air disarmament of German occupied territories (May 1945-June 1946)
> AIR 20/9843-9845 Air Division: GAF disbandment (1944-1945)

Initially, BAFO comprised four Group headquarters: No 2 Group was largely a bomber Group; Nos 83 and 84 had fighter and reconnaissance roles; and No 85 was a support Group. Records for these Groups can be found in AIR 25, and station records in AIR 28. A number of the stations used played important roles during the war when in German hands. For example, Sylt and Jever were employed as Luftwaffe fighter bases (AIR 28/1510 and AIR 28/1219-1221 respectively). At the end of 1945, BAFO contained thirty-six operational squadrons, but, as with the rest of the RAF, the Command contracted during 1946, so that by the following year only ten squadrons remained in BAFO. The operations of the various squadrons can be followed in squadron records in AIR 27.

An occupation force of ten squadrons might have sufficed had Europe set on a course of peaceful reconstruction, but this was not to be the case. Fundamental differences between the Western Allies and the Soviets which were evident in the closing stages of the Second World War widened after 1945. While the Western powers had reduced their forces on the Continent to less than one quarter of the VE Day strengths, the Soviets maintained their forces on a war footing. The Cold War started in earnest in February 1948, when the Soviets engineered a Communist takeover of Czechoslovakia. Four months later, the Soviets blockaded Berlin, by closing all the road, rail and water routes linking West Berlin with the three western zones controlled by Britain, France and the USA. The only means of keeping two million West Berliners alive was to transport the food, coal and other raw materials to Berlin by air using the three air corridors which linked the west of the city to the western zones. Code-named Operation 'Vittles' by the USAF, and Operation 'Plainfare' by the RAF, the 'Berlin Airlift', as it became known, lasted, in effect, until September 1949, and during that time over 2,000,000 tons of supplies reached Berlin in 277,728 sorties. Seventy-six per cent of the total tonnage was delivered by the USAF, seventeen by the RAF, and the remainder by civilian aircraft.

The single most important document on Operation 'Plainfare' is to be found in AIR 10/5067. This is a large Air Publication, No 3257, entitled *A report on Operation Plainfare (the Berlin Airlift)*, by Air Marshal T M Williams, C-in-C of BAFO, dated April 1950. The report is so comprehensive that it was decided in the 1950s that an official narrative was not required. However, those wishing to do additional work should look also at Berlin Airlift Progress Reports contained in AIR 8/1647-1650, 1658. Other interesting examples of 'Plainfare' material include AIR 20/7148 Operation 'Plainfare' (1948-1951), AIR 20/7071 Air Supply of Berlin: Civilian Aviation Contribution (1948-1949), and AIR 15/816-817 Coastal Command Activities: Operation 'Plainfare' (1948-1949). An interesting post-airlift file is AIR 8/1855 Berlin - Air Safety Talks with Russians (1953-1954).

Especially after the blockading of Berlin, the British Chiefs of Staff based their plans on the assumption that the Soviet Union would be the principal adversary in the next major war. The occupation role of the RAF, as with the other British Services in Germany, was now less appropriate than had originally been the case, and BAFO's duties were changing in response to the creation in 1949 of the North Atlantic Treaty Organization (NATO). Relatively few NATO files are available, but those that exist are in AIR 20 and AIR 8. The following is a cross-section:

> AIR 20/9787 Allied Air Forces Central Europe and Continental Air Defences (1957-1958)

AIR 20/10614 Deployment of Missiles in NATO (1960)
AIR 8/1806 Development of Western Democratic Alliance (1951)
AIR 8/2000 European Defence Force: Possible RAF Role (1952)
AIR 8/2064-2067 NATO Reappraisal and Political Directive (1956-1957)
AIR 8/1853 Revised NATO Force Requirements (1953)
AIR 8/1652 NATO war reserves - aircraft and aircrew (1951)

By the early 1950s, it was felt that the conventional forces of NATO had been run down too far, and in the face of massively larger Eastern Bloc forces, moves were made to improve western nuclear capability. Great Britain's contribution was the 'V' Force.

The history of Great Britain's nuclear deterrent is complex, and because of the paucity of primary material available, you are strongly advised to consult secondary works before approaching the records. Some of the better books on the subject are the following:

Arnold, L, *A Very Special Relationship: British Atomic Weapons Trials in Australia*, HMSO, 1987
Brookes, A J, *V-Force: the History of Britain's Airborne Deterrent*, Jane's, 1982
Gowing, M, *Independence and Deterrence: Britain and Atomic Energy, 1945-1952*, Vol I: *Policy Making*, Vol II: *Policy Execution*, MacMillan, 1974
Pierre, A J, *Nuclear Politics: The British Experience with an Independent Nuclear Force*, Oxford University Press, 1972

One of the RAF's participants in the first tests at Christmas Island in 1957 was Air Vice-Marshal Wilfrid Oulton, and his recollections are recounted in *Christmas Island Cracker: An Account of the Planning and Execution of the British Thermo-Nuclear Bomb Tests, 1957*, Thomas Harmsworth, 1987.

These secondary sources provide a useful background to the research and development of Britain's nuclear weapons. Those interested in the technicalities of the early devices can look at some of the Air Publications released in AIR 10, such as AIR 10/7675 Atomic Weapons: Basic Physics, Radiation and Detection (1961), and AIR 10/8622 BLUE STEEL: Guidance, control and navigation systems (1963-1966). Some of the earliest files are contained in AIR 8, and among the most interesting are AIR 8/2309 Nuclear weapons - testing (1952-1962), AIR 8/2308 Report on Monte Bello testing (1952). AIR 8 also contains information on the deployment of nuclear weapons within NATO. Another class of documents which contains nuclear files is AIR 20. Many of these relate to squadrons involved in the Christmas Island tests, and a major Operation 'Grapple' section can be found in AIR 20/10391-10458 (respectively The preparatory phase: joint administrative plan (1956) Meteorological reports (1956-1958). Other files include AIR 20/9334 No 24(C) Squadron in Operation GRAPPLE (1956-1959), AIR 20/10355 Operation GRAPPLE: organization and administration: formation of No 160 Wing (1956-1957)), and AIR 20/10380 No 206 Squadron: Operation GRAPPLE X (1957). Another nuclear file of interest is AIR 20/8559 Operation of fighter aircraft in radioactive fallout (1956-1958).

The squadrons involved in the main test programme between 1952 and 1958 can be identified from the secondary sources and files in AIR 20. It must be emphasized, however, that very few Operations Record Books (ORBs) relating to these squadrons are open for the period 1952 to 1958.

Aircraft and related technology

One of the features of the late 1940s was the expanding research into the jet engine by Sir Frank Whittle and other British scientists. The Whittle papers are contained in AIR 62, and include files which cover the late 1940s, such as AIR 62/2 Notes on development of jet propulsion (1935-1949). Research by the firm English Electric led to one of the great success stories of British aviation after 1945: the Canberra. It was the world's first jet medium bomber, entering service with the RAF in May 1951. By the mid-1950s, the RAF had over 250 Canberras, and in 1958 the aircraft was given nuclear capability. The Canberra's early development is covered in AIR 8/1518 The Canberra - development (1950-1952), and operational trial work is recorded in AIR 14 (such as AIR 14/4064 Operational trials in FEAF (1956-1957)). Other Canberra files are in AIR 20, including AIR 20/9873 Canberra polar flights (1954-1955). The early Canberras achieved some notable aviation records, including the winning of the London-New Zealand Air Race in October 1953 (AIR 8/1732 England/New Zealand Air Race), and a new record between London and Cape Town in December 1954 (AIR 20/9887 Report on Canberra flight to South Africa (1954)). The aircraft was built in twenty different marks, and was exported in large numbers, seeing service with the Australian, New Zealand and Canadian air forces. See, for example, AIR 8/1687 Canberras for RCAF (1951). The Canberra was even made under licence in the USA for service with the USAF (AIR 20/7101 Canberra aircraft production in America (1950-1951)).

While jet aircraft development was forging ahead in the late 1940s, the RAF was still dependent upon Second World War vintage aircraft, or developments of these aircraft, such as the Shackleton (which grew out of the Lancaster). Ways of extending the service life of many piston engined aircraft were investigated by the Central Bomber Establishment (CBE) and the Central Fighter Establishment (CFE) (AIR 63 and AIR 64 respectively). The CBE, formed in September 1945 and disbanded four years later, tested a variety of bomber aircraft, including the Lancaster and the Lincoln (AIR 63/36 Lincoln aircraft - basic performance trial (1948)). There were trials of Second World War equipment, further developed for post-war service (AIR 63/19 H2S Mark III in Lancaster aircraft (Oct 1947)). The CFE, formed in 1944 and disbanded in 1966, performed similar types of work, including comparisons between piston engined and jet aircraft (AIR 64/74 Tactical trials - Meteor III: comparison with Tempest V (1946)), and trials of the latest jet fighters (AIR 64/1-158 Tactical trials of the Hunter Mks.I-VI (1954-1958)). The CFE also made comparisons between Allied and enemy aircraft, such as AIR 64/169 F 86 versus MiG-15. Other material on the piston engined aircraft is sprinkled throughout AIR 20: for example, AIR 20/9287 Report on Shackleton intensive flying trials (1951), and AIR 20/9751 Flying, technical and handling instructions - Shackleton Mk III (1957-1960).

The creation of the V-Force dominated the 1950s, and aircraft development in the period concentrated on the types which were to deliver Britain's nuclear device. Most of the material relating to the V-Force bombers can be found in AIR 14 and AIR 20, and the following is a sample for each aircraft:

> AIR 20/7469 Valiant Production: Vickers-Armstrongs Ltd Report (c. 1949)
> AIR 14/4069 Introduction of Valiant aircraft into Bomber Command (1953-1956)
> AIR 20/9723-9727 Valiant: Test Flight Reports (1953-1959)
> AIR 14/4059-4064 Victor Mk II, Victor B Mk II, Vulcan - intensive flying trials. Narrative reports (1961-1962)

Other files are in AIR 8. AIR 8/2315 deals with Victor/Vulcan development and production (1951-1966).

AIR 8 and AIR 20 contain material which relates to aircraft development in general in the post-war period, and some of the more valuable items are:

> AIR 20/6948 Fighters: policy (1948-1951)
> AIR 20/6954 Transport aircraft: policy (1949-1955)
> AIR 20/6955 Maritime aircraft: policy (1949-1955)
> AIR 20/6800 Re-equipment of squadrons: Coastal Command (1947-1954)
> AIR 20/7019 Bomber production: policy (1947-1951)
> AIR 20/8211 Bomber Production and Development (1949-1954)
> AIR 20/7036 Training aircraft: policy (1949-1952)

AIR 20 also contains material on foreign aircraft, such as AIR 20/10284 Evaluation of foreign aircraft (1954-1956). A substantial number of files relating to the development of the various aircraft categories can also be found in the respective Command classes (AIR 14 Bomber Command, AIR 15 Coastal Command, AIR 16 Fighter Command, etc).

Those interested in the technical side of aviation should look at AVIA classes, especially AVIA 6 Royal Aircraft Establishment (records up to 1950) and AVIA 8 Air Ministry Research and Development. AVIA 19 contains the reports of the Marine Aircraft Experimental Establishment (MAEE). Established in 1924 and closed in 1956, the MAEE investigated the performance of water-based aircraft. AIR 10 (Air Publications) also has material on individual aircraft and equipment, such as AIR 10/6790 Shackleton GR Mk I (1950-1963) and AIR 10/5394 Vulcan: Airframe equipment (1954).

Developments relating to Army airborne operations and transport operations are covered in AIR 66 Joint Air Transport Establishment: Reports. AIR 67 is a continuation of this series, and contains drawings of equipment used in such roles.

Those who wish to follow the operational performance of aircraft should also look at squadron ORBs (AIR 27), having identified squadrons either in the primary records or in secondary works, such as Owen Thetford's *Aircraft of the Royal Air Force since 1918*, Puttnam and Co, London, 1988.

Another major repository of aircraft material is the Royal Air Force Museum, Department of Research and Information Services, Hendon, London NW9 5LL.

Overseas operations

The Malayan Emergency, 1948-1960: Operation 'Firedog'

While the Berlin Airlift was under way, Britain became committed to a campaign in the Far East which has since been regarded as a model for conducting counter-insurgency warfare. During the Second World War, the Allies had supplied arms and equipment to guerrilla units fighting the Japanese in South-East Asia. In Malaya, the main guerrilla effort was organized by the Malayan Communist Party (MCP). At the end of the war, the MCP refused to hand back their weapons, and in June 1948 launched the second phase of their campaign - the liberation of Malaya from British control. Attacks were made on civilians (both Malay and British), and rubber plantations and tin mines (which laid the foundations of the Malay economy) were destroyed.

Operation 'Firedog' was the civilian and military campaign which aimed at isolating the communist terrorists from local support. The role of the Far East Air Force, with its headquarters at Singapore and bases in Malaya, was one of support for the police, army and civilian government. Intelligence information was the key to success, and Auster and Pioneer aircraft undertook the vital low level reconnaissance. Transport aircraft, Valettas and Dakotas, kept the troops in the jungle supplied, and also carried out leaflet dropping operations. Offensive air strikes were performed by a variety of aircraft, including Spitfires and Beaufighters. The first use by the RAF of helicopters in a combat zone came in April 1950 with the creation of the Casualty Evacuation Flight, which was based at RAF Seletar in Singapore using Dragonflies. Later in the campaign, the helicopters were used for troop carrying. The Malayan Emergency ended officially in 1960 after the Malay Peninsula was declared safe.

By far the best introduction to the subject is a comprehensive official history of the air campaign entitled *The Malayan Emergency, 1948-1960*, by Malcolm Postgate, which can be found in AIR 41/83. The work has recently been published by HMSO under the title *Operation Firedog: Air Support in the Malayan Emergency, 1948-1960* (1992). For those with a general interest in the air campaign in Malaya, this work should be sufficient as a source. It has an impressive array of annexes, ranging from Ground and Air Forces Orders of Battle to the number of sorties flown by each type of aircraft involved. However, if you require greater detail, you will find most of the material relating to Operation Firedog in AIR 23 and, to a lesser extent, AIR 20. The following is a selection:

> AIR 23/8435 Reports (annual) on the RAF operations in Malaya (1948-)
> AIR 23/8443-8444 Reports on operations in Malaya (1948-1952)
> AIR 23/8620-8622 Defence of Malaya against an increased internal threat (1952-1954)
> AIR 23/8437 'The Role of the RAF in Malayan Bandit War', prepared for BDCC (1950-1951)
> AIR 23/8441 Reports on air strikes carried out by aircraft from Singapore (1949-1951)
> AIR 20/10376 Review of the emergency in Malaya from June 1948 to August 1957 (1957)
> AIR 20/8925-8928 Director of Operations Committee - Meetings, Agenda (1951-1954)

The operations of the various RAF squadrons involved in Operation 'Firedog' can be examined in greater depth by looking at the squadron ORBs in AIR 27, using the official history (AIR 41/83) mentioned above to identify the squadrons. Some general higher policy material may be found in AIR 24 Commands for the Far East Air Force, although a number of files relating to Air HQ Malaya remain closed. AIR 24/2274-2280 are open, and cover 1950s operations. See also AIR 8, including AIR 8/1615 The strategic position of Malaya, including report by the Joint Planning Staff (1947-1948), and AIR 8/1629 Malaya: Air Effort (1950-1956).

The Korean War, 1950-1953

Because of commitments in Malaya, Great Britain made only a limited contribution to the Korean War. The United Nations decided to give military support to the South Koreans when they were invaded by North Korean forces in June 1950. UN forces were primarily American, but the British Commonwealth provided the third largest contingent. The North Koreans were defeated, but in the winter of 1950-1951 Chinese intervention led to a bitter campaign and a stalemate on the 38th parallel until an Armistice was agreed in July 1953.

The RAF element of the British forces was small. The only RAF aircraft to see operational service were three Sunderland squadrons, which were employed for maritime reconnaissance patrols against seaborne incursions and other activity along the coast. Based at Seletar in Singapore and Iwakuni (southern Japan), the Sunderlands flew both by day and by night, often in hazardous sub-zero weather conditions. The operations of each of the squadrons are covered in the ORBs: AIR 27/2440 No 88 Squadron (1946-1954); AIR 27/2461 No 205 Squadron (1946-1950) and AIR 27/2660 (1951-1954); and AIR 27/2467 No 209 Squadron (1946-1950) and AIR 27/2663 (1951-1954). For a more general view see, in particular, AIR 8/1504 Detachment of Sunderland Squadrons (1950-1951) and AIR 20/7412 Sunderland operations and maritime warfare policy (1950-1955).

RAF personnel served with USAF and Royal Australian Air Force (RAAF) units on an individual basis, some thirty men serving with No 77 (RAAF) Squadron, and a total of twenty-seven RAF personnel were killed in Korea. RAF officers also contributed to the war in an advisory capacity, the two most prominent being Wing Commander (later Air Vice-Marshal) 'Johnnie' Johnson, and Wing Commander (later Air Vice-Marshal) Peter Wykeham. The former had been on loan to the USAF since 1948, advising on air combat techniques, and the latter was sent to Korea in 1950 as an expert on fighter-intruder operations. Early in the Korean campaign the Americans realised that they had neglected night ground attack tactics, in particular, and Peter Wykeham, who had commanded units operating over North Africa, Italy and Germany, was sent to the Fifth Tactical Air Force. One of his memoranda can be found in AIR 20/7796 Five reports on tactical aviation in Korea (Jan 1951), Report No 5, 'The Planning and Operation of Night Intruder Aircraft'. Other material on operational tactics includes AIR 20/7313 Reports on operations: tactics, techniques, etc (1950-1952), and AIR 20/8929 Various analytical reports (1951-1955).

At the higher command level, the RAF had some input in the form of Air Vice-Marshal Sir Cecil Bouchier, who was Senior British Liaison Officer in General MacArthur's headquarters in Japan. There is a whole class devoted to Bouchier's correspondence in DEFE 33 Korean War: Chiefs of Staff Liaison: Tokyo Reports. Additional Bouchier material can be found in AIR 8/1608, which contains communications between Bouchier and General MacArthur in the period July to September 1950. AIR 20/8804 contains Directives to Bouchier between 1950 and 1952. The AIR 24 Commands series has Far Eastern Air Force HQ files relating to the Korean period.

Among the interesting items on Korea are comparisons of aircraft performance. At the start of the war, some units flew Meteors until it was seen that the aircraft was outclassed by MiG-15s of the Chinese Air Force. See AIR 8/1709 MiG-15/Meteor Combats (1951-1952). Other comparisons were made between MiG-15s and Sabres, AIR 20/7728 MiG-15 versus F 86E. See also Central Fighter Establishment (AIR 64) files for comparisons (AIR 64/169 is one example). An interesting assessment of the opponent is in AIR 8/1708 Communist Air Power (1951).

A good general introduction to the subject is provided in Air Chief Marshal Sir David Lee's book *Eastward: A History of the Royal Air Force in the Far East, 1945-1972* (HMSO, 1984).

Kenya, 1952-1956: the Mau Mau Rebellion

In the emergency created by the Mau Mau rebellion, the RAF operated in a role similar to that in Malaya, but on a vastly reduced scale. Indeed, aircraft resources were so scarce that Harvard trainers fitted with machine-guns were pressed into service in support of ground troops. They were supplemented by a small number of ground attack Vampires and Bomber Command Lincolns. Few files of note remain, and the following comprise the more important ones: AIR 8/1886 Air operations in Kenya (1954-1955); AIR 20/9529 Report on Mau Mau operations - Kenya, November 1953 (1954), and AIR 14/4071-4073 Operations in Kenya - intelligence aspect (1953-1955).

Suez, 1956: Operation 'Musketeer'

The Suez crisis was initiated by Egypt's abrogation in October 1954 of a treaty which permitted the British use of bases in the Canal Zone until 1956, with the possibility of extensions beyond that date. A withdrawal to Cyprus and Aden was made, and these became the major centres of British military presence in the Middle East. In the summer of 1956, a number of months after the withdrawal had been completed, a major crisis broke. There was evidence of communist bloc military aid to Egypt, and the Egyptian government announced that it intended to nationalize the Suez Canal, in retaliation for the withdrawal of US and British financial backing for the Aswan Dam project. Britain and France, which also had commercial and strategic reasons for wanting freedom of movement in the Suez Canal, concentrated their naval, military and air forces on Malta and Cyprus. After the failure of diplomacy, Operation 'Musketeer' was launched at the end of October 1956, comprising a British and French seaborne invasion of the Canal Zone, supported by parachute forces.

The RAF's role in Operation 'Musketeer' was to attack Egyptian airfields and prevent the MiG-15 fighters and Il-28 bombers of the Egyptian air force from interfering with the main invasion force. Canberras and Valiants carried out high-altitude bombing, and low-flying Canberras, Venoms and French aircraft completed the destruction of the Egyptian air force within two days. Hastings and Valettas, meanwhile, dropped British paratroops. The operation was a success militarily, and there were relatively few casualties. RAF losses were three officers and one airman killed. However, because of diplomatic pressure, a withdrawal became necessary.

An introduction to the subject can be found in Air Chief Marshal Sir David Lee's book *Wings in the Sun: a History of the Royal Air Force in the Mediterranean, 1945-1986* (HMSO, 1989). Within PRO classes, most 'Musketeer' material is in AIR 8 and AIR 20, and the following is a representative sample:

    AIR 8/1940 Operation MUSKETEER: general papers (1956-1958)
    AIR 8/1948 Suez Canal crisis: planning for military operation MUSKET
        EER (1956)
    AIR 8/2083 Suez Canal crisis: command arrangements and directives
        (1956)
    AIR 8/2097 Operation MUSKETEER: sitreps (1956)
    AIR 8/2111 MUSKETEER: air operations (1956-1957)
    AIR 20/10203-10204 Operation MUSKETEER: bomber operations (1956)
    AIR 20/10206 Operation MUSKETEER: directives and operational orders
        (1956)

AIR 20/10214 Operation MUSKETEER: air operations (1956)
AIR 20/10215 Operation MUSKETEER: targets (1956)

Among the more interesting files is AIR 20/10371 MUSKETEER: counter meas-
ures against lies and exaggerated reports (1956). Some higher level material
relating to Suez can be found in AIR 24 Commands in the files of HQ Middle
East Air Force, AIR 24/2465-2467, and in the files of Air HQ Malta (AIR 24/
2528, in particular). Two bases on Malta (Luqa and Hal Far) and two on Cyprus (Nicosia and Akrotiri) were used during 'Musketeer', and the available
ORBs for these are:

AIR 28/1307 Luqa (1955-1956)
AIR 28/1318 Akrotiri (1955-1960)
AIR 28/1322 Nicosia (1956-1958)

Cyprus, 1956-1960: the EOKA Emergency

Cyprus, which was the main base for the launching of the Suez operations,
was troubled by a campaign of violence by the Greek Cypriot EOKA guerrillas
between 1956 and 1960. As in the Malayan Emergency, helicopters were used
in support of ground troops, and proved their worth in hunting terrorists in
the mountains. One unit, No 284 Squadron, employing Sycamores, pioneered
the techniques of night flying and of landing troops using scrambling ropes.
In addition, the unit dropped food and ammunition, as well as evacuating
some 200 people from upland areas. The squadron was widely hailed as having made the principal contribution to routing the guerrillas. Its ORB is in AIR
27/2853 (1956-1959).

The strategic importance to Great Britain of Cyprus is discussed in a number of
AIR 8 files, including AIR 8/10328-10329 Cyprus: sovereignty and strategic
importance (1959-1960). Internal security and the monitoring of the guerrillas
are areas covered in AIR 8/1921-1923 (1956-1958).

Once again, David Lee provides useful background to the RAF's participation
in Cyprus in his book *Wings in the Sun*, Chapter 8.

Indonesian 'Confrontation', 1963-1966

British armed forces were once more called to South-East Asia when the newly
created Malaysia confederation (comprising Malaya, Singapore, Sabah and

99

Sarawak) was threatened by Indonesia. The territorial aspirations of Indonesia had long encompassed these areas. The flashpoint was Borneo, and the Indonesians provided support for rebel groups who were opposed to the concept of Malaysia. Rebellion flared up in Brunei, a British Protectorate, in December 1962, supported by a Borneo Liberation Army, which was, in turn, supported by Indonesia. The political and operational details are outlined by David Lee in his *Eastward* book, and it is sufficient here to mention in short that the RAF's contribution to the British response was the air defence and reconnaissance of Malaya, Singapore and Borneo. Ground attack Hunters were deployed from Singapore to North Borneo, and helicopters (Whirlwind, Wessex and Belvedere) and short range transports (Beverley and Pioneer) provided mobility for the British, Commonwealth and Malayan troops. Detachments of Canberras and V-bombers were also sent to Singapore to act as deterrents.

Relatively few documents on the Indonesian 'Confrontation' are, as yet, available in the PRO, because of the dates involved. Most significant of those which have been released is AIR 8/2441 Malaysian/Indonesian Confrontation, 1962-1966: Official History (1969-1972). This 'in-house' history (from the CAS's department) is a useful starting point for research, and should provide a basic reference point as other material becomes available. Other recently released files include:

> AIR 8/2437-2440 Malayan area: defence arrangements (1962-1963)
> AIR 8/2443 Malaysia: air defence (1963-1964)

Personnel

General

The post-war cuts in defence spending and the restructuring of defence policy inevitably led to a decline in the numbers of officers and men required in the RAF. At its peak post-war strength, in 1952, the total manpower was 270,000, and one-third of this number were National Servicemen. A decade later, the figure was 148,000.

The main features of post-war manpower policy are covered in AIR 20 files, and chiefly under Code 68. General policy files include:

> AIR 20/6559-6563 Strength of the Armed Forces and Service Estimates, 1947-1948 (1946-1948)
> AIR 20/7177 RAF Manpower: Policy (1947-1949)
> AIR 20/9129 Strength of post-war armed forces (1946)

AIR 20/9055 Manpower Economy Committee: second interim report
(1947-1952)

AIR 20/9057 Manpower: strength of armed forces, including correspondence with Prime Minister on manning of RAF (1948-1952)

AIR 20/10915 RAF Manpower (1950-1958)

Files relating to National Service are also found in AIR 20 Code 68, and the
following is a sample:

AIR 20/9204 Manpower: policy for National Service (1946-1953)

AIR 20/8993 Manpower: rate of intake of National Service entrants (1947-
1949)

AIR 20/9066 Reduction in period of National Service from 18 months to
12 months (1951-1953)

AIR 20/8671 National Service: selection, allocation, effect on industry,
training (1953-1954)

Policy concerning particular aircrew and ground trade categories can also be
found in AIR 20. Among the more interesting are:

AIR 20/6439 The economical utilization of aircraft, aircrews, maintenance
personnel (1946)

AIR 20/6457 The Attitudes of Serving Airmen: report of working party,
compiled from survey in UK and BAFO (1948)

AIR 20/7393 Aircrew: policy including future requirements, conditions
of eligibility, size limitations and medical standards required in
modern warfare (1949-1955)

AIR 20/7615 Age limit for fighter pilots (1951-1952)

AIR 20/9045 Policy for commissioning of aircraft captains and crew (1944-
1949)

AIR 20/9064 Flying personnel: pilots and navigators - general policy
papers (1950-1954)

Records of service

When researching the record of service of an individual who served in the
RAF, you should approach the Personnel and Training Command, RAF
Innsworth, Gloucester GL3 1EZ in the first instance. Officers' Records of Service are held by Department PG 5a(2), and Airmen by Department P Man 2b(1).
Details from a record of service will be released only to next of kin, or with
their permission, and in all cases a non-refundable fee (£15 at the time of publication) is charged in advance. Information provided in a record of service

allows you to identify the units with which an individual served, and, from here, you can go to the unit histories concerned (AIR 27 Squadrons, AIR 29 Miscellaneous Units, etc).

Honours and awards

Enquiries regarding campaign medals and awards for gallantry can be also be made to the MOD Personnel Management Centre. You should refer to Department S10J (AIR) for gallantry medals, and Department PMan 3d(4) for campaign medals.

It is possible to find some general policy files relating to the award of gallantry and campaign medals in AIR 8. One of these deals with the Suez operation: AIR 8/2125 Suez Canal dispute (Operation MUSKETEER): honours and awards (1957). However, it appears that most files on post-war campaign and bravery medals no longer survive.

Casualties

One of the first tasks facing the RAF at the conclusion of the Second World War was the tracing of personnel who were recorded as Missing on Operations. After VE Day and VJ Day, RAF investigation teams were sent into former enemy territory in an endeavour to establish the fate of such personnel. A history of their efforts is in AIR 2/10031 Missing Research and Enquiry Service (MRES): History (1948-1950). See also AIR 2/9910 MRES.: long term policy (1947-1952).

The MRES passed on information on casualties to the Commonwealth War Graves Commission (CWGC), who have the responsibility for graves of Commonwealth servicemen and other nationalities who died while in service with the RAF. In cases where no grave was known for a serviceman, his name was recorded on one of a number of memorials tended by the CWGC depending on the theatre of operations in which he was lost. The MRES and the CWGC continued their work after the Second World War, and were involved in a number of post-war conflicts, including Korea. However, as time passed, it became more usual to have deceased servicemen repatriated, and the functions at one time performed by the CWGC are now undertaken by the Personnel Management Centre PM 3(a). Enquiries to the CWGC can be made at the following address: 2 Marlow Road, Maidenhead, Berks SL6 7DX. The Personnel Management Centre, PM 3(a), is at RAF Innsworth, Gloucester GL3 1EZ.

The CWGC and the Personnel Management Centre are able, in most cases, to give a date of death and unit. However, when more details surrounding a loss are required, the Ministry of Defence Air Historical Branch (RAF) may be able to assist. The AHB holds both wartime and post-war casualty lists, but it must be emphasized that priority is given to next of kin enquiries, and all enquiries must be in writing, to the following address: MOD Air Historical Branch (RAF), 3-5 Great Scotland Yard, Whitehall, London SW1A 2HW.

Post-war Air Ministry/Ministry of Defence structure

The defence body as a whole underwent a number of changes in the late 1940s. The first of these to affect the Air Ministry was the handing over of responsibility for civil aviation to a new Ministry of Civil Aviation in 1946. The changing defence scene in the late 1940s led to the creation of a Ministry of Defence to co-ordinate the policy of the three Services.

The creation of a Ministry of Defence had less of an impact upon the RAF than may be imagined, as the Air Ministry continued as the body in charge of the air force. However, within the new establishment, each Service was subjected to close scrutiny by various reviewing committees in an attempt to exact economies.

In 1948 a committee was appointed to review the organization of the Air Ministry. Its findings, which led to a more streamlined Air Staff body and a clearer definition of air force policy, are in AIR 20/6587 Report of a Committee appointed to revise the organization of the Air Ministry (May 1949). Among the committee's findings was the lack of what were described as 'firm policy decisions' for the future. The implied criticism was that the Air Ministry was still, in the late 1940s, preoccupied with winding down the wartime strength, rather than thinking ahead. The report also pointed to what the committee regarded as over-specialization in Air Ministry organization, saying that wartime expedients were not only being carried over into the peacetime structure, but that these were being built upon. The creation in 1945 of the Air Member for Technical Services (AMTS) was seen as an unnecessary development. This post took over the functions of the old Air Member of Training. The changes to the Air Ministry's structure in the immediate post-war years are covered in AIR 20/7163 Reorganization of the Air Staff (1946-1947). In response to the 1949 report, the post of AMTS was disestablished, and his functions were taken over by the Air Member for Supply and Organization (AMSO). The implementation of the committee's recommendations is reported upon in AIR 20/6588 Air Staff economies arising from the Quig Report (1949-1950).

Another committee was appointed in 1957 to review the organization of the Air Ministry 'in the light of prospective commitments, and in the interests of economy'. The committee's findings were issued in March 1958, and appear in AIR 20/10531. The call for a new review of Air Ministry organization was prompted by the 1957 Statement on Defence, which comprehensively reshaped defence policy. The new policy, constructed by Duncan Sandys, emphasized the value of ballistic missiles as a deterrent force, and put an effective end to large-scale British research into supersonic manned bombers, and fighter aircraft of types more advanced than the Lightning. The policy was modified in subsequent years when developments in missile technology fell below expectation, but the damage done to the British aircraft industry was irrevocable. See AIR 8/2200 Future of the Aircraft Industry (1957-1962).

The next significant change came in April 1964, when the functions of the Air Ministry, Admiralty and War Office were all completely absorbed into a reconstituted Ministry of Defence. Thus, after forty-six years, the Air Ministry ceased to exist.

Other AIR classes which contain material on the post-war Air Ministry structure and the various defence debates are AIR 2 and AIR 8. AIR 2/9738, for example, covers Air Ministry organization proposals put forward in 1947-1948, and Code 7/1 covers post-war developments generally. In AIR 8 there are a number of 'size and shape of the armed forces' files, including AIR 8/1587-1589 for the years 1947-1950. Some compiled in the period of the Sandys statement are worth noting:

> AIR 8/2156 Future Organization of Defence Services: Report (1957)
> AIR 8/2157 Defence White Paper and Defence Debate (1957)
> AIR 8/2063 Economies in defence expenditure (1956)
> AIR 8/2166 Defence Policy, 1958/9: Effect of possible cuts (1957-1958)

AIR 20 also has occasional Air Ministry organization files, one of the most valuable being AIR 20/6958 Reorganization of the Air Staff - policy (1946-1958).

The Chief of Air Staff was the RAF's representative on the Chiefs of Staff Committee. CAB 79 contains material up to the end of 1946, and DEFE 4 covers the period from 1947.

Post-war Women's Royal Air Force

The question of whether the three Women's Auxiliary Services should be retained as regular forces after the war was considered by the War Cabinet as early as January 1943. An inter-departmental committee was formed under the chairmanship of Ralph Assheton, Financial Secretary to the Treasury, and it concluded that the three Women's Services would be required after hostilities ceased.

The subject was discussed again in the course of 1944 by Air Ministry Post-War Planning and Manning committees. Although there were concerns over the cost of a regular Women's Auxiliary Air Force (WAAF), the introduction of a voluntary extended service scheme to cover the immediate post-war shortage of manpower was suggested. This was agreed to by Cabinet, and on 30 May 1946 the Government announced that the Women's Services would be retained on a regular voluntary basis. The terms of the scheme were published in an Air Ministry Order in November 1946. It was stated that the WAAF would be incorporated in the RAF, with an appropriate change of title; it would be constituted on the same basis as the RAF as far as duties and trades were concerned, and would be governed by RAF regulations, modified as necessary.

As with the RAF, the WAAF was affected by demobilization. From a total of 97,744 officers and airwomen in January 1946, the Service was pared down to 20,142 two years later. In 1948, however, it became evident that there were going to be serious shortages in a number of branches and trades, and so a special Short Service Scheme was introduced in July of that year. Otherwise, periods of service for officers were for three, four or five years from the date of appointment on the active list, with reserve service given for those below five years on the active list. Service for airwomen was for two, three or four years, without a liability for reserve service.

The immediate post-war period, between 1946 and 1949, was one of transition. Many officers and airwomen extended their service, and many rejoined the WAAF after short spells in civilian life.

A decision was made in 1948 to rename the WAAF, in order to reflect its regularized status, and the Women's Royal Air Force (WRAF) came into being officially on 1 February 1949.

The researcher who is interested in the WAAF, or WRAF, will be disappointed by the paucity of official accounts. Air Publication 3234 *Women's Auxiliary Air Force*, which is found in AIR 10/5546, covers the war period adequately, but the addition of a post-war section, which is shortly to appear in the PRO, is of little value outside the years 1946-1949. The gap is not filled by academic works on the subject, and the best overall view is provided by the anecdotal book by Squadron Leader Beryl Escott, *Women in Air Force Blue: the Story of Women in the Royal Air Force from 1918 to the Present Day* (Wellingborough, Patrick Stephens, 1989). However, some material can be found in AIR 2 and AIR 6. For example, the reports of the Assheton Committee are in AIR 2/7824 Future of the Women's Services: Appointment of Inter-departmental Committee (1943-1947); post-war pay and conditions are covered in AIR 2/7825 Post-war pay, allowances and pensions: position of the Women's Services (1946-1947); and the outcome of high level discussions can be found in Air Council Conclusions in AIR 6 (see, for instance, AIR 6/75 Air Council Conclusions (January 1944 to December 1945), which deals with the extended service scheme).

The Fleet Air Arm

With the amalgamation of the Royal Naval Air Service and the Royal Flying Corps in 1918, the RAF assumed responsibility for both land-based and carrier-borne maritime aviation. However, neither maritime aspect was to flourish. Financial constraint, the Air Ministry's championing of strategic bombing doctrine, and inter-Service rivalry, centring on a dispute between the navy and the air force over the control of naval aviation, meant that maritime aviation did not advance very far during the inter-war period. The naval aviation controversy so dominated inter-departmental business that there was no important co-operation between the navy and the air force in maritime air research, and it required the arbitration of a succession of governmental committees before the dispute was settled.

The complexities of the dispute over naval aviation are dealt with by the official historian Stephen Roskill in *Naval Policy between the Wars*, Vols I and II (London, Collins, 1968-1976), and the official narrative history 'The RAF in Maritime War' found in AIR 41/45, and you should consult these works before approaching the primary record. As the Air Ministry controlled naval aviation for most of the inter-war period, the dispute is most easily approached from AIR classes, although you need to look at ADM files to appreciate the problem from the Admiralty's perspective. The largest collections of material on the subject are found in AIR 8 and AIR 9. Some of the earliest exchanges between the departments are in AIR 8/17 (including correspondence between the Admiralty and the Air Council in 1919), and AIR 8/30 (including Parliamentary debates on the subject). Trenchard's controversial 1921 paper, in which he proposed that the air force should be considered a substitute for the navy, is in AIR 8/45 Substitution of Air Force for other forces in Imperial Defence (1921-1930). Other relevant files in the series include AIR 8/66 CID Sub-Committee on Relations between the Navy and the Air Force (1923), AIR 8/78 Navy, Army and Air Force Expenditure: Colwyn Committee (1925-1926), AIR 8/79 Naval Controversy, 1925-1926: Prime Minister's Arbitration (1925-1926). Among the AIR 9 files, AIR 9/2 FAA and Naval Co-operation (1924-1936) is the most important, covering twelve years. This contains much of the Air Ministry's first writings on the big ship controversy. More general memoranda are to be found in AIR 9/5 Separate Air Force controversy (1917-1936). Another AIR class which deals the subject is AIR 5. See especially AIR 5/6 Relations between the Air Force and the Navy (1923-1930). Among the ADM series, ADM 116/1836 has useful material on the Admiralty's early objections to Air Ministry control over naval aviation.

A *modus vivendi* between the Admiralty and the Air Ministry was achieved by the end of the 1920s, but the effective resolution of the naval aviation dispute did not occur until 1937, when the Prime Minister appointed the Minister for Co-ordination of Defence, Sir Thomas Inskip, to look into the issue after the Admiralty renewed its claim to FAA units. A copy of the Inskip Report is in AIR 8/223 (1937). See also AIR 8/229 FAA: transfer of responsibility to the Admiralty: papers (1937-1939), and AIR 8/211-212 FAA (1936). Another collection of relevant papers is in CAB 16 Committee of Imperial Defence: Ad Hoc Sub-Committees, CAB 16/151 and 152. From the Admiralty's perspective, see ADM 1/10107 FAA: transfer of administrative control from Air Ministry to Admiralty (1937-1939), and ADM 1/10127 FAA: transfer to naval control (1939).

In spite of the financial constraints and inter-Service wranglings of the 1920s and 1930s, the FAA achieved some notable successes. It had been agreed between the Admiralty and the Air Ministry at the conclusion of the First World War that, while the RAF would maintain ultimate control over FAA units, the Admiralty was free to employ FAA aircraft as it saw fit within the confines of Fleet action. The Admiralty expressed its determination to continue with aircraft carrier experimentation, and regular exercises with the Fleet were organized for the FAA. Analyses of trial work with the Fleet can be found in the following sample:

> AIR 9/7 Air Staff notes (1918-1928)
> AIR 8/85 Bombs, torpedoes and anti-aircraft gunnery: notes (1926-1928)
> AIR 2/201 Torpedo aeroplane attack in Atlantic Fleet exercises (1920)
> AIR 2/1910 FAA Torpedo Trials; effectiveness of anti-aircraft fire (investigations of CID sub-committee) (1936-1938)
> AIR 2/1071 Night attack on Fleet (1923-1935)

In addition to the above, some operational records for the period after April 1933 are in AIR 27/2387. This piece comprises ORBs for the following squadrons: 701, 720, 801-803, 805, 806, 812, 813, 815, 816, 819, 821, 823-826, 828 and 841.

The FAA had some forty-six squadrons and 230 aircraft when the Royal Navy took formal control in May 1939, and when hostilities commenced four months later, carriers were deployed with the East Indies, South Atlantic, Home and Mediterranean Fleets. Initially, aircraft carriers were used in anti-submarine work, but the early loss of *Courageous* (17 September 1939) changed this policy, and thereafter most FAA work involved the provision of air cover for surface operations. Nevertheless, losses among the carriers continued to be high until the mid-war point: *Glorious* (June 1940), *Ark Royal* (November 1941), *Hermes* (April 1942), and *Eagle* (August 1942). There were, however, some important victories for the FAA. On 11 November 1940 there was the courageous attack on the Italian Fleet at Taranto by Swordfish from the *Illustrious*. In May 1941 Swordfish from the *Ark Royal* and the *Victorious* disabled the *Bismarck*, allowing the finishing blows to be delivered by the Royal Navy's capital ships. Later in the war, FAA units operated with considerable success in an anti-shipping role, both in the Mediterranean and off Norway, including operations against the *Tirpitz*. After VE Day, the FAA served with the British Pacific Fleet. ADM 1 has interesting pre-war policy material concerning the anticipated role of the FAA, such as ADM 1/9720 Role of FAA in event of European War (1938). See also ADM 1/9721 State of FAA on 1 April 1939 (1938-1939).

The main FAA operational records for the Second World War are in ADM 207 FAA Squadrons. Each of the squadrons has the equivalent of an ORB, and front-line squadrons are denoted by 800 series allocations. In some cases, records for individual FAA squadrons are sketchy, and you will need to consult the records of the carriers in which the units were embarked. A good example of this is the FAA action against the *Bismarck* in May 1941; the operations of the Swordfish squadrons involved (Nos 818 and 820) are most easily traced via the *Ark Royal*'s record in ADM 199/657. Other operational records can be found under Code 90 (Aviation) of ADM 1 Admiralty and Secretariat Papers, ADM 116 Admiralty and Secretariat Cases, and ADM 182 Admiralty Fleet Orders. It is also worth looking at ADM 199 War History Cases and Papers. Within AIR classes, AIR 27/2387 has records up to September 1943, and AIR 27/2386 records up to 1946. AIR 50 (Combat Reports) contains some supplementary material. This class contains reports which were made by Allied aircrew to their Intelligence Officers on returning from operations, and the items relevant to the FAA are AIR 50/320-331, covering the years 1940-1944. ADM 1 has some material on specific operations. For example, the attack on Taranto is dealt with in ADM 1/11182 FAA attack on Taranto (1940-1941).

As far as ADM series are concerned, records for the post-war years follow the same format, although you should note that many of the classes end in the late 1950s (ADM 182 goes to 1958, ADM 207 to 1957, ADM 219 to 1959, and ADM 291 to 1953). Within ADM 1, aviation records after 1951 are organized according to a file's year of registration. Within each year, the documents are arranged alphabetically according to Branch prefix. For example, A refers to Air Branch, AA Aircraft Accidents, AWD Air Warfare Directorate, etc. In addition to these, some FAA material may be found under PD Plans Directorate and OD Operations Division.

The FAA was involved in many of the major post-war conflicts also involving the RAF, and two of the most significant were Korea and Suez. Unfortunately for the researcher, many of the records relating to post-war operations such as these remain closed. However, it is possible to find some operational material by looking for references to the carriers involved. The FAA operated in a total of five carriers at various stages of the Korean conflict (*Theseus, Triumph, Ocean, Glory* and *Sydney*), and some documents relating to these five can be found in ADM 1, for example, ADM 1/23260 Air Combat reports from HMS *Ocean*: Sea Fury and Firefly aircraft against enemy MiG15s (1952-1953). In cases where the FAA operated overseas, it is possible to find relevant ADM 1 references under Code 52 Foreign Countries, such as ADM 1/22364 HMS *Theseus* action in Korean War: details of operations (1951-1952), and ADM 1/22368 Korean Operations: report on employment of No 14 Carrier Group (1951). More general documents are also elsewhere in ADM 1, such as ADM 1/23259 F86 Sabre operations: report by Lieut Cdr J S Bailey of experiences with USAF fighter wing in Korea (1952-1954), and ADM 1/24068 Carrier operations off Korea: threat of Soviet built jet bombers (1951-1953). The Suez operation was notable for the fact that it was the first occasion on which the FAA used jet aircraft in combat. Sea Hawks and Sea Venoms were deployed from the carriers *Albion, Bulwark* and *Eagle*, while helicopters were used for commando assault operations for the first time from *Ocean* and *Theseus*. Among the significant non-combative roles for the FAA at the time was involvement in Operation 'Grapple'. The carrier *Warrior* was deployed as a floating airfield during the 1957 test programme at Christmas Island. Very few references to Suez and Operation GRAPPLE are available to public view, but some general information may be found in documents such as ADM 1/26720 Aircraft Carrier Squadron Memoranda (1956-1957).

A small number of references to the post-war FAA and naval aviation are be found in AIR files. Among the more significant are AIR 8/2135 Role and composition of the Royal Navy and Fleet Air Arm (1956-1960), AIR 8/1592 Naval aviation and maritime air forces (1950), AIR 8/2445-2447 Aircraft carriers and intervention, and threat to shipping studies (1965), and AIR 20/11423 Future aircraft carriers and the island strategy: Admiralty/Air Ministry (1963). Other relevant material can be found in AIR 65 Air/Sea Warfare Development Unit: Reports. The ASWDU grew out of the Coastal Command Development Unit, and its function was to conduct tactical and weapons trials on behalf of Coastal Command and the FAA. The class includes minutes of the Naval Air Tactical Conference at Lee-on-Solent in 1948. Other ASWDU files are in AIR 20 (see, for example, AIR 20/6812 Air/Sea Warfare Development Unit - policy (1948-1951). It is also advisable to look at AVIA classes for naval aviation references. For instance, AVIA 6/17229-17237 contains Royal Aircraft Establishment reports on the Naval Air Department's Research and Development programme between 1957 and 1962.

Fleet Air Arm aircraft and related technology

If you are interested in technical developments within the FAA you should look at a number of other ADM series. For example, ADM 264 consists of Air Ministry publications which relate to naval aircraft and their installations. ADM 219 comprises operational research papers dating from 1942, and among the relevant files are ADM 219/95 Achievements of British and US escort carriers (1944), and ADM 219/112 A comparison between Swordfish and Avenger aircraft (1944). Another source is ADM 234, which contains printed books and pamphlets issued to the Navy in the Books of Reference series. ADM 291 contains the reports of the RN Aircraft Repair Yard, Fleetlands. Nor should ADM 1 be overlooked. This class has aircraft and technical references sprinkled throughout. See, for example, ADM 1/10103 Fleet Air Arm: aircraft types required (1933-1939), ADM 1/10747 Experimental and new aircraft for FAA (1936-1940), ADM 1/10106 FAA: trials of Fairy Seafox (1936-1938), and ADM 1/11961 Instrument and Blind Approach (1941-1944). The provision of American aircraft (such as the Avenger) under Lend/Lease provisions is dealt with in ADM 1/11938 Aircraft provided for FAA under Lend/Lease arrangements (1942).

Another repository of FAA material is the Fleet Air Arm Museum, Royal Navy Air Station, Yeovilton, Somerset BA22 8HT. It is equipped especially to deal with aircraft queries.

Fleet Air Arm personnel: records of service

The records of service of FAA personnel are held by the Ministry of Defence, CS(R)2, Bourne Avenue, Hayes, Middlesex UB3 1RF. Information is provided usually only to next of kin, or when permission has been granted by them, and in all cases a non-refundable fee (£15 at time of publication) is charged in advance.

Secondary sources

In addition to the official history *Naval Policy between the Wars* by Stephen Roskill mentioned above, other useful secondary works which deal with the FAA are: Geoffrey Till, *Air Power and the Royal Navy, 1914-1945: A Historical Survey* (London, Jane's, 1979), which is another sound academic piece; Ray Sturtivant, *The Squadrons of the Fleet Air Arm* (London, Air Britain, 1984), regarded by many as the best reference work; and Paul Beaver, *Encyclopaedia of the Fleet Air Arm since 1945* (Wellingborough, Patrick Stephens, 1987).

Organization of the Air Council to 1949

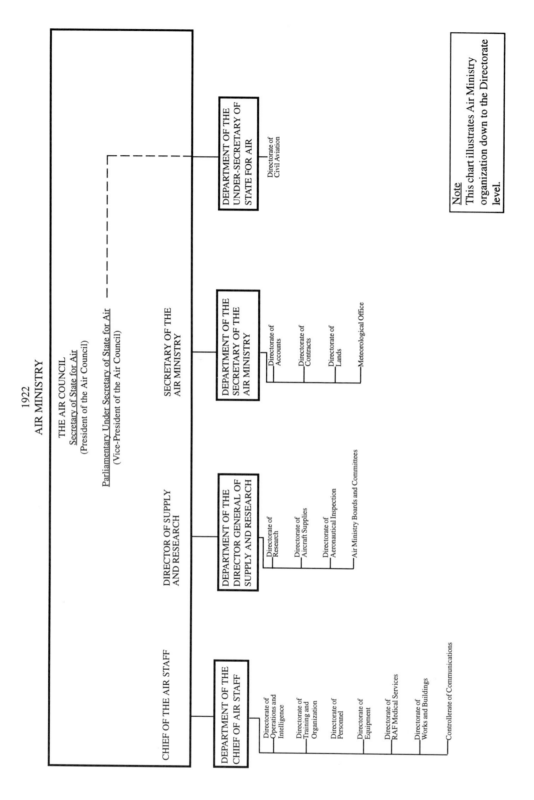

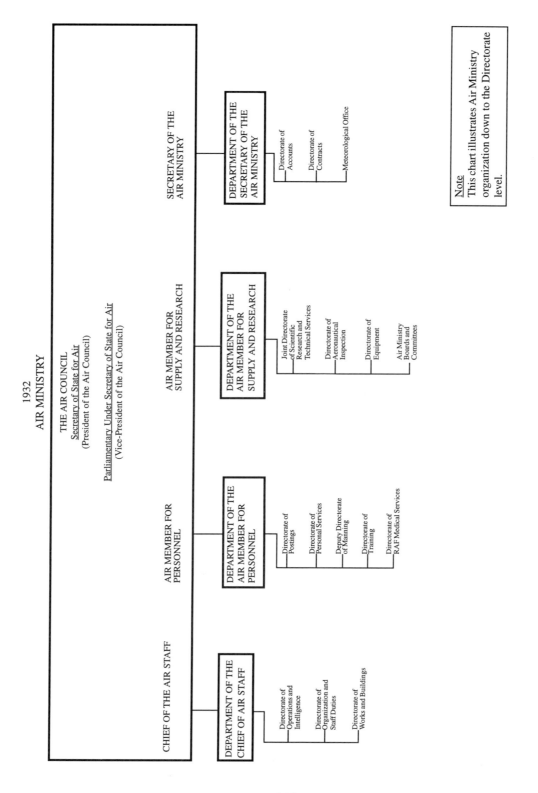

1932
AIR MINISTRY

THE AIR COUNCIL
Secretary of State for Air
(President of the Air Council)

Parliamentary Under Secretary of State for Air
(Vice-President of the Air Council)

CHIEF OF THE AIR STAFF

AIR MEMBER FOR PERSONNEL

AIR MEMBER FOR SUPPLY AND RESEARCH

SECRETARY OF THE AIR MINISTRY

DEPARTMENT OF THE CHIEF OF AIR STAFF
- Directorate of Operations and Intelligence
- Directorate of Organization and Staff Duties
- Directorate of Works and Buildings

DEPARTMENT OF THE AIR MEMBER FOR PERSONNEL
- Directorate of Postings
- Directorate of Personal Services
- Deputy Directorate of Manning
- Directorate of Training
- Directorate of RAF Medical Services

DEPARTMENT OF THE AIR MEMBER FOR SUPPLY AND RESEARCH
- Joint Directorate of Scientific Research and Technical Services
- Directorate of Aeronautical Inspection
- Directorate of Equipment
- Air Ministry Boards and Committees

DEPARTMENT OF THE SECRETARY OF THE AIR MINISTRY
- Directorate of Accounts
- Directorate of Contracts
- Meteorological Office

Note
This chart illustrates Air Ministry organization down to the Directorate level.

113

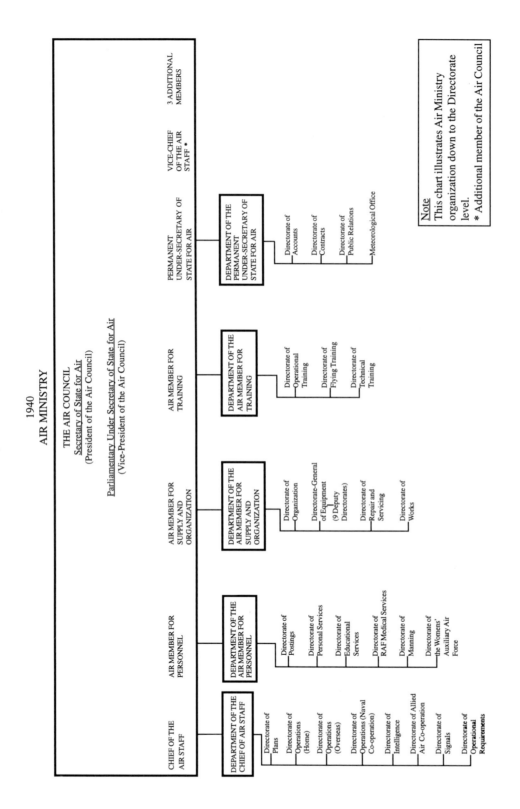

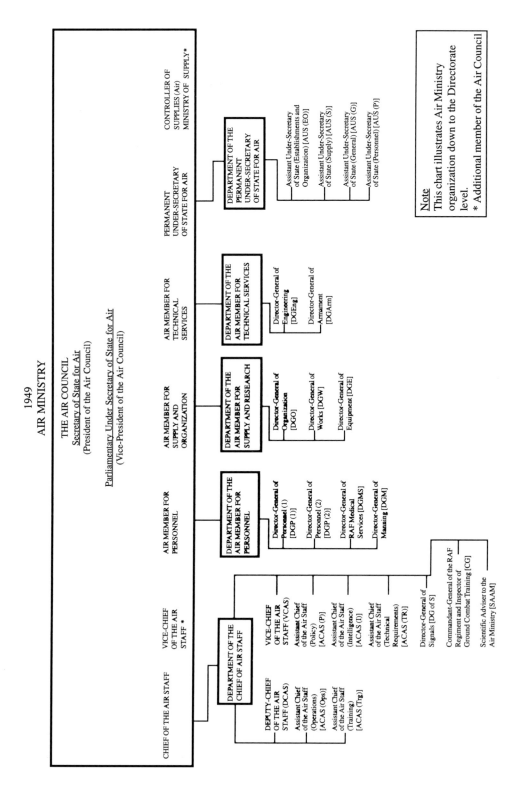

1949
AIR MINISTRY

THE AIR COUNCIL
Secretary of State for Air
(President of the Air Council)

Parliamentary Under Secretary of State for Air
(Vice-President of the Air Council)

| CHIEF OF THE AIR STAFF | VICE-CHIEF OF THE AIR STAFF * | AIR MEMBER FOR PERSONNEL | AIR MEMBER FOR SUPPLY AND ORGANIZATION | AIR MEMBER FOR TECHNICAL SERVICES | PERMANENT UNDER-SECRETARY OF STATE FOR AIR | CONTROLLER OF SUPPLIES (Air) MINISTRY OF SUPPLY * |

DEPARTMENT OF THE CHIEF OF AIR STAFF

VICE-CHIEF OF THE AIR STAFF (VCAS)

DEPUTY-CHIEF OF THE AIR STAFF (DCAS)

Assistant Chief of the Air Staff (Operations) [ACAS (Ops)]

Assistant Chief of the Air Staff (Policy) [ACAS (P)]

Assistant Chief of the Air Staff (Training) [ACAS (Trg)]

Assistant Chief of the Air Staff (Intelligence) [ACAS (I)]

Assistant Chief of the Air Staff (Technical Requirements) [ACAS (TR)]

Director-General of Signals [DG of S]

Commandant-General of the RAF Regiment and Inspector of Ground Combat Training [CG]

Scientific Adviser to the Air Ministry [SAAM]

DEPARTMENT OF THE AIR MEMBER FOR PERSONNEL

Director-General of Personnel (1) [DGP (1)]

Director-General of Personnel (2) [DGP (2)]

Director-General of RAF Medical Services [DGMS]

Director-General of Manning [DGM]

DEPARTMENT OF THE AIR MEMBER FOR SUPPLY AND RESEARCH

Director-General of Organization [DGO]

Director-General of Works [DGW]

Director-General of Equipment [DGE]

DEPARTMENT OF THE AIR MEMBER FOR TECHNICAL SERVICES

Director-General of Engineering [DGEng]

Director-General of Armament [DGArm]

DEPARTMENT OF THE PERMANENT UNDER-SECRETARY OF STATE FOR AIR

Assistant Under-Secretary of State (Establishments and Organization) [AUS (EO)]

Assistant Under-Secretary of State (Supply) [AUS (S)]

Assistant Under-Secretary of State (General) [AUS (G)]

Assistant Under-Secretary of State (Personnel) [AUS (P)]

Note
This chart illustrates Air Ministry organization down to the Directorate level.
* Additional member of the Air Council

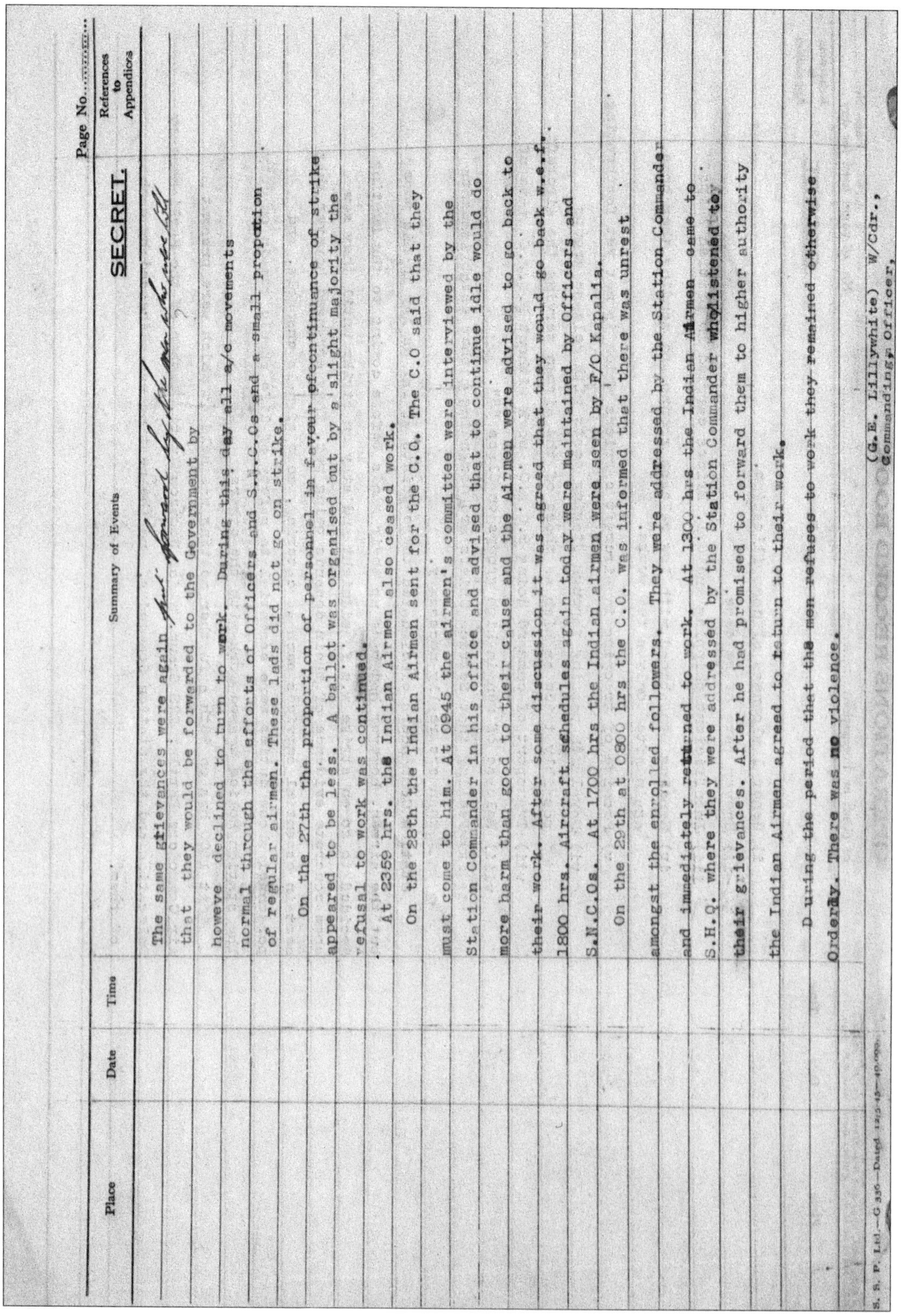

Page No.............

Place	Date	Time	Summary of Events	References to Appendices

SECRET

The same grievances were again put forward by the men who ask [?] that they would be forwarded to the Government by howeve declined to turn to work. During this day all a/c movements normal through the efforts of Officers and S.N.C.Os and a small propotion of regular airmen. These lads did not go on strike.

On the 27th the proportion of personnel in favour of continuance of strike appeared to be less. A ballot was organised out by a slight majority the refusal to work was continued.

At 2359 hrs. the Indian Airmen also ceased work.

On the 28th the Indian Airmen sent for the C.O. The C.O said that they must come to him. At 0945 the airmen's committee were interviewed by the Station Commander in his office and advised that to continue idle would do more harm than good to their cause and the Airmen were advised to go back to their work. After some discussion it was agreed that they would go back w.e.f. 1800 hrs. Aircraft schedules again today were maintained by Officers and S.N.C.Os. At 1700 hrs the Indian airmen were seen by F/O Kapalia.

On the 29th at 0800 hrs the C.O. was informed that there was unrest amongst the enrolled followers. They were addressed by the Station Commander and immediately returned to work. At 1300 hrs the Indian Airmen came to S.H.Q. where they were addressed by the Station Commander who listened to their grievances. After he had promised to forward them to higher authority the Indian Airmen agreed to return to their work.

During the period that the men refuses to work they remained otherwise orderly. There was no violence.

(G.E. Lillywhite) W/Cdr.,
Commanding Officer,

S. S. P. Ltd.—G 336—Dated 1145-45-40,000

figure 26: Operations Record Book for RAF Dum Dum, 24 January 1946: strikes in Singapore (AIR 28/199)

Part of the Operations Record Book of RAF Dum Dum near Calcutta for January 1946, showing the 'strike' on the 24th of the month by airmen who complained that their rate of demobilization was far slower than other groups of service men.

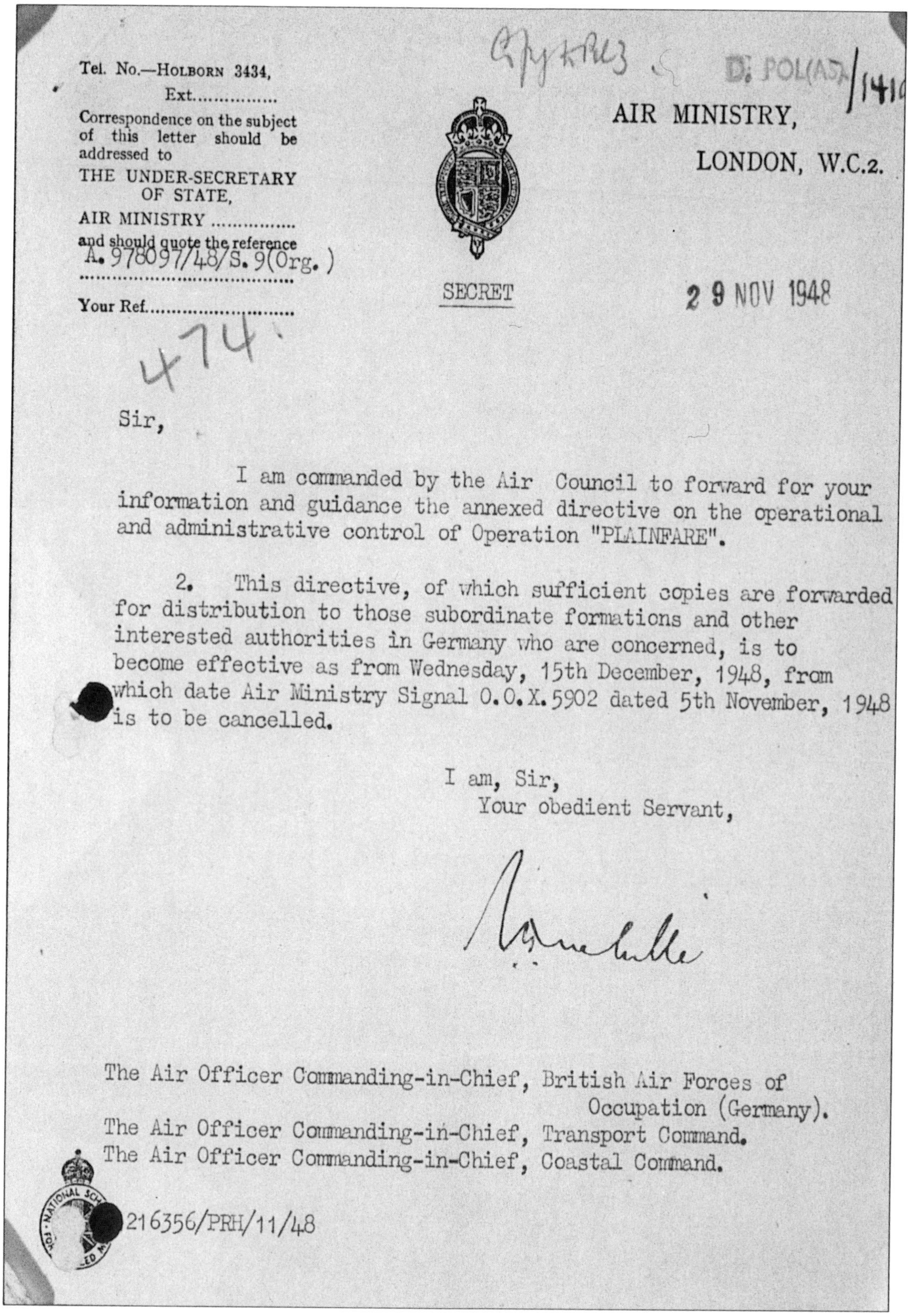

Tel. No.—HOLBORN 3434.

Ext.................

Correspondence on the subject of this letter should be addressed to

THE UNDER-SECRETARY OF STATE,

AIR MINISTRY ....

and should quote the reference
A. 978097/48/S. 9(Org.)

....

Your Ref.........................

474

AIR MINISTRY,

LONDON, W.C.2.

SECRET

2 9 NOV 1948

Sir,

I am commanded by the Air Council to forward for your information and guidance the annexed directive on the operational and administrative control of Operation "PLAINFARE".

2.   This directive, of which sufficient copies are forwarded for distribution to those subordinate formations and other interested authorities in Germany who are concerned, is to become effective as from Wednesday, 15th December, 1948, from which date Air Ministry Signal O.O.X.5902 dated 5th November, 1948 is to be cancelled.

I am, Sir,
Your obedient Servant,

The Air Officer Commanding-in-Chief, British Air Forces of
Occupation (Germany).
The Air Officer Commanding-in-Chief, Transport Command.
The Air Officer Commanding-in-Chief, Coastal Command.

216356/PRH/11/48

figure 27: Operation 'Plainfare': letter to the Secretary of State on the Berlin Airlift, 29 November 1948 (AIR 20/7148)

This letter from the Air Ministry, together with its accompanying directive, was issued at the height of Operation 'Plainfare', the airlift into Berlin which began in June 1948 after the Russians brought to a halt all surface communications from the West to Berlin. The blockade was lifted on 12 May 1949, but the British and the Americans continued their airlift for almost four more months in order to build up stockpiles in Berlin.

R.A.F. Form 540

See instructions for use of this form in K.R. and A.C.I., para. 2349, and War Manual, Pt. II, Chapter XX and notes in R.A.F. Pocket Book.

OPERATIONS RECORD BOOK

of (Unit or formation) ___No. 6 Squadron___

Page No. 1

No. of pages used for day

Place	Date	Time	Summary of Events	References to Appendices
AKROTIRI	NOVEMBER 1st	1956	1. OPERATIONS. After all the preparation, anticipation, and waiting, we at last saw action today. During the night allied bomber aircraft were employed against Egyptian military targets, and from dawn throughout the day the Venom Wing here at Akrotiri was operating against Egyptian airfields adjacent to the Suez Canal. The first Venom aircraft to strike Egypt were a section of eight led by Squadron Leader ELLIS, our Squadron Commander. Taking off at 0515 hours, they were on target at "S" hour which was 0604 hours local time. Attacking Kasfareet and Kabrit, they encountered no enemy aircraft in the air, and the only opposition was very meagre and innaccurate light anti aircraft fire. Two MIG 15s were destroyed and an unidentified piston engined aircraft damaged. Heartened by the reports of the first section, the subsequent missions took off in high spirits, morale being very high throughout the Squadron. In all thirty four sorties were flown today, including one by Group Captain MACDONALD, the Station Commander. 13 Egyptian aircraft were destroyed and 15 damaged. The airfields attacked were Kasfareet, Kabrit, Fayid, Abu Sueir, and Shallufa. Three hangars were destroyed and four left burning, further ones being sprayed with cannon fire. Buildings, fuel bowsers, and soft skinned vehicles were also attacked. A large number of MIG 15s were found at Abu Sueir when the first section, led by Flight Lieutenant HARRISON, arrived there on the second wave. Indeed seven of them were destroyed by our four Venoms, and a further two were damaged. There were still many left dispersed round the airfield when the section left. On the way to the target, this section encountered two MIG 15s seventy miles from the Cyprus coast. The MIG 15s apparently did not see our section which did not give chase because of the carriage of full external fuel tanks and rocket projectiles. To jettison these would have meant an abortive mission. As from today, each operational mission had as its callsign a form delta number; and G.45 recorder cameras were used. The films from these were most unsatisfactory, the pictures being badly defined. We think that this was caused by dust and condensation on the camera pod window, the latter occuring during the rapid descent into the target area. Throughout the operations the aircraft continued	

6970/PMKC/8-43

figure 28: Operations Record Book for No 6 Squadron at RAF Akrotiri, 1 November 1956: Suez crisis (AIR 27/2727)

The Anglo-French dispute with Egypt over the Suez Canal resulted in open warfare at the end of October 1956. This began with Operation 'Musketeer' on 31 October, when Valiants from Malta and Canberras from Malta and Cyprus launched high-level attacks against Egyptian airfields. These were followed on 1 November with ground attacks by Venoms from Cyprus, such as those shown in this Operations Record Book of 6 Squadron at Akrotiri. After four days of these and other air attacks the Egyptian Air Force was neutralised.

figure 29: Gloster Javalin FAW 6 at RAF Stradishall, 1957 (AIR 28/1424)
Gloster Javalin FAW 6 serial XA836, photographed at Stradishall in Suffolk on
30 September 1957, was the first of this variant to be delivered to 89 Squadron.
The Javalin FAW 1 entered service with the RAF in February 1956 and was the
first twin-jet fighter in the world, capable of high performance in all weathers.

figure 30: Vickers Valiant refuelling a Javalin, 1960 (AIR 19/1004)
Vickers Valiant B1 serial XD816, converted to the tanker role, of 214 Squadron at
Marham in Norfolk, refuelling Gloster Javalin FAW 7 serial XH887. This photo-
graph accompanies the Air Estimates file of 1960/61.

figure 31: Blue Steel Missile attached to an Avro Vulcan, 1960 (AIR 19/1004)

A Blue Steel, the strategic air-to-surface missile made by Hawker Siddeley Dynamics, being loaded for trials on Avro Vulcan B1 serial XA903. Vulcans first entered service with Bomber Command in July 1956 and Blue Steels first became operational in February 1963. This photograph accompanies the Air Estimates file of 1960/61.

Appendixes

Appendix 1:

Secretaries of State for Air 1918-1964

Lord Rothermere	Jan-Apr 1918
Sir William D Weir	Apr 1918-Jan 1919
W S Churchill	Jan 1919-Apr 1921
F E Guest	Apr 1921-Nov 1922
Sir Samuel Hoare	Nov 1922-Jan 1924
C B (later Lord) Thomson	Feb-Nov 1924
Sir Samuel Hoare	Dec 1924-June 1929
Lord Thomson	June 1929-Oct 1930
Lord Amulree	Oct 1930-Nov 1931
Marquess of Londonderry	Nov 1931-June 1935
Sir Philip Cunliffe-Lister (Viscount Swinton from Jan 1936)	June 1935-May 1938
Sir Kingsley Wood	June 1938-Feb 1940
Sir Samuel Hoare	March-May 1940
Sir Archibald Sinclair	June 1940-May 1945
M H MacMillan	June-July 1945
Viscount Stansgate	July 1945-Sept 1946
P J Noel-Baker	Oct 1946-Sept 1947

A Henderson	Sept 1947-Oct 1951
Lord de L'Isle and Dudley	Oct 1951-Dec 1955
N C Birch	Jan 1956-March 1957
G R Ward	Apr 1957-July 1960
J Amery	Aug 1960-Apr 1962
H C P J Fraser	May 1962-Apr 1964

Chiefs of Air Staff 1918-1963

Sir Hugh Trenchard	1 Apr 1918
Sir Frederick Sykes	12 Apr 1918
Sir Hugh (later Lord) Trenchard	31 Mar 1919
Sir John Salmond	1 Jan 1930
Sir Edward Ellington	22 May 1933
Sir Cyril Newall	1 Sept 1937
Sir Charles Portal	25 Oct 1940
Sir Arthur Tedder	1 Jan 1946
Sir John Slessor	1 Jan 1950
Sir William Dickson	1 Jan 1953
Sir Dermot Boyle	1 Jan 1956
Sir Thomas Pike	1 Jan 1960
Sir Charles Elworthy	1 Sept 1963

Appendix 2:

RAF Aircraft Damage Categories Pre-1952

Pre-1941	Cat.U	Undamaged
	Cat.M(u)	Capable of being repaired on site by the operating unit
	Cat.M(c)	The repair is beyond unit capacity
	Cat.R(B)	Repair on site is not possible; the aircraft must be dismantled and sent to a repair facility
	Cat.W	Write-off
1941-1952	Cat.U	Aircraft undamaged
	Cat.A	Aircraft can be repaired on site
	Cat.Ac	Repair is beyond the unit capacity (ie may be repaired on site by another unit or contractor)
	Cat.B	Beyond repair on site (ie repairable at a Maintenance Unit or at a contractor's works)
	Cat.C	Allocated to Instructional Airframe duties

Cat.E	Aircraft is a write-off
Cat.E1	Aircraft is a write-off but is considered suitable for component recovery
Cat.E2	Aircraft is a write-off and suitable only for scrap
Cat.E3	Aircraft is burnt out
Cat.Em	Aircraft is missing from an operational sortie (Missing aircraft categorized 'Em' after 28 days)

In addition to the above, the cause of the damage is sometimes indicated by a prefix or suffix, thus:

FA   Flying Accident
FB   Operational Loss
GA   Ground Accident
T   Technical Cause
EA   Enemy Action

For comparison, the following table indicates the major equivalent classifications:

Pre-1941	1941-1952	1952-1961
U	U	1
M(u)	A	2
M(c)	Ac	3
R(B)	B	4
-	C	5(gi)
W	E	5
-	E1	5(c)

| - | E2 | 5(s) |
| - | Em | 5(m) |

The 1952-1961 damage classification system introduced Categories 1 to 5 with a number of additional sub-categories. A modified version of this system is in use today. For details of both of the post-1952 systems see: *Roundel* (British Aviation Research Group), Vol 3 (June 1993), pp 59-61.

Appendix 3: Sources of RAF and other aerial photographs

This appendix describes some of the locations where photographs associated with RAF activities can be found in Britain.

Public Record Office

The holdings of the PRO include a wealth of RAF and other aerial photographs, which usually accompany related documentary material in various records. A very large catalogue of these photographs has already been built up, and can be found in the Reference Room. It has been continuously extended as further photographs come to light, and you are invited to complete forms (available from the staff on request) to show the whereabouts of any that you find in the course of your researches. The catalogue is in five ledgers, divided into three sections:

> Photographs Index: Subjects: Parts I and II provide an alphabetical list in which, for example, you can find the lettercode, class and piece references for:
> > Accidents: Air
> > Aerial Bombing
> > Aerial Combat
> > Air Defence
> > Aero Engines
> > Aircraft Markings
> > Air Intelligence
> > Aircraft Production
> > German Air Force
> > Hiroshima
> > Royal Air Force Stations

> Photographs Index: Persons, Places is a single ledger which lists the contents in alphabetical order so that, for example, you can find the lettercode, class and piece references for:
> > under Persons:
> > > Bader, Gp Capt D
> > > Gibson, Wg Cdr G P
> > > Harris, ACM Sir A T
> > > Tedder, Lord
> > > Trenchard, Lord

under Places [relating to aerial references]:
> Aleppo, Palestine
> Freidburg, Germany
> Le Creusot, France
> Nicosia, Cyprus
> Valetta, Malta

<u>Photographs Catalogue: Parts I and II</u> provide a cross-reference by listing the photographs in alphanumeric order under lettercode, class and piece numbers. Some notable references where photographs can be found are:

AIR 1	Air Historical Branch Records: Series I. Contains some excellent photographs, but you must expect a lengthy hunt through the piece numbers. Examples are in AIR 1/2269-2279.
AIR 5	Air Historical Branch Records: Series II. Contains records of the airship R101 under code 42/1.
AIR 11	Royal Airship Works, Cardington. Contains photographs of various balloons and non-rigid airships.
AIR 27	Squadron Operations Record Books. Where interesting photographs were taken in the air or on the ground, copies were sometimes pasted in these books. For example, under AIR 27/1509 you can find numerous photographs taken during daylight attacks by Beaufighters of 252 Squadron from June 1944 to the end of the war in the Eastern Mediterranean.
AIR 28	Stations Operations Record Books. In addition to including photographs in their records, Stations sometimes devoted whole books to them. An example is AIR 28/733, in which RAF St Eval compiled an Appendix of photographs taken from January 1940 to November 1942.
AIR 34	Contains a very large selection of photographs, mostly taken during the Second World War by air reconnaissance units such as the Photographical Development Unit which was formed at the outbreak of the war, the photographic Reconnaissance Units which were formed from July 1940 and the various RAF and USAAF Reconnaissance Squadrons which were formed from February 1943 onwards. These photographs were interpreted

by units in the UK which were combined into the Central Interpretation Unit in January 1941, becoming the Allied Central Interpretation Unit in May 1944. This became the Joint Air Photographic Intelligence Unit in August 1947 and was renamed the Joint Air Reconnaissance Intelligence Centre in December 1953. In addition, other Interpretation Units were formed abroad. However, many of the wartime photographs have been passed to the University of Keele, as shown below.

AIR 40   Directorate of Intelligence contains some photographs of German aircraft and airfields in the Second World War.

AIR 59   Director of Works is devoted to photographs of various stages of construction of airship sheds, aeroplane hangars and seaplane bases.

AIR 60   Directorate of Research contains photographs of aircraft, airships, balloons, equipment and accessories.

AIR 62   Whittle Papers contain photographs of the development of the jet engine by Air Cdre Sir Frank Whittle.

AVIA 30   National Gas Turbine Establishment includes Whittle drawings and negatives of various gas turbine jet engines and their components.

BT 220   Civil Aviation: Accident Investigation Branch includes photographs of crashed aircraft and wreckage.

CN 5   consists solely of photographs extracted from AIR classes.

CN 6   consists solely of photographs extracted from AVIA classes.

SUPP 9   Consists solely of British and American military and naval aircraft.

WO 319   War of 1914-1918: Palestine Campaign consists solely of photographs of terrain and towns in the Middle East.

WO 323   War of 1914-1918: Italian Campaign consists solely of photographic panoramas of the Alpine region near the Austrian border.

University of Keele
Air Photo Library, Department of Geography, Newcastle-under-Lyme,
Staffordshire ST5 5BG

This University houses about five million photographs taken by reconnaissance aircraft from November 1939 to May 1945. They cover Germany, parts of German-occupied Western Europe and the north shore of the Mediterranean Sea. There is no cover of the United Kingdom, nor of those countries which remained neutral during the Second World War. These photographs are stored here under s. 4(1) of the Public Records Act 1958. Requests for specific areas should state the name of a site or a neighbouring settlement and its position to the nearest minute of latitude and longitude. Facilities are also provided within the Department for consultation, provided that sufficient notice is given and a suitable date can be arranged.

Imperial War Museum
Lambeth Road, London SE1 6HZ

This large collection of photographs, which is housed in All Saints' Annexe, concentrates mainly on the First and Second World Wars. It includes most aircraft types, action photographs taken in the air and others showing daily life on the ground, including some of well-known aviators. There is an excellent collection of reconnaissance photographs of trenches in the British sector in the First World War. There is a smaller but useful inter-war collection. The collection after the Second World War has gaps, but there are photographs of the Falklands War and others of air operations in the Gulf War. Most of the photographs are in viewing albums which can be seen by appointment.

Royal Air Force Museum
Grahame Park Way, Hendon, London NW9 5LL

The collection comprises some 250,000 prints, negatives and transparencies. It includes some aircraft types from the early days to the present time, as well as many airfields and a few shots taken in action. The Charles E Brown collection is remarkable, consisting of a comprehensive range of Second World War aircraft in colour. Most of the photographs are in viewing albums which can be seen by appointment.

National Library of Air Photographs
RCHME, National Monuments Record Centre, Kemble Drive, Swindon, Wiltshire SN2 2GZ

This library, part of the Royal Commission on the Historical Monuments of England, houses several million air photographs which provide a unique and comprehensive record of the English landscape from the earliest days of flying to the present day. About 500,000 of these are oblique photographs illustrating architectural, archaeological and landscape subjects. The remainder of vertical air photographs derive from RAF, Ordnance Survey and commercial sources, mostly from 1940 onwards. Vertical photographs were usually taken with a fore and aft overlap of about sixty per cent so that pairs of photographs can be viewed stereoscopically, giving a 3-D image. Written applications for searches may be made, or personal visits arranged by appointment.

Addresses for smaller collections of aerial photographs held are:
RCAHM (Wales), Eddeston House, Queens Road, Aberystwyth, Dyfed SY23 2HP
RCAHM (Scotland), John Sinclair House, 16 Bernard Terrace, Edinburgh EH8 9NX
RCAHM, Lire Building, The University, Newcastle upon Tyne, Tyne and Wear NE1 7RU (holds black and white vertical surveys of the North of England, duplicating those held at the Swindon site).

For a fuller list of collections, readers are advised to consult the *NAPLIB Directory of Aerial Photographic Collections in the United Kingdom 1993*, published by Aslib, The Association for Information Management, Information House, 20-24 Old Street, London EC1V 9AP.

Bibliography

Adkin, Fred, *From the ground up: a history of RAF ground crew*, Shrewsbury, 1983

Arnold, L, *A Very Special Relationship: British Atomic Weapons Trials in Australia*, London, HMSO, 1987

Beaver, P, *Encyclopaedia of the Fleet Air Arm since 1945*, Wellingborough, Patrick Stephens, 1987

Boyle, Andrew, *Trenchard*, London, 1962

Brookes, A J, *V-Force: the History of Britain's Airborne Deterrent*, London, Jane's, 1982

Bruce, Jack M, *The Aeroplanes of the Royal Flying Corps (Military Wing)*, London, Puttnam, 1982

Craven, Wesley F, and Cate, James L, *The Army Air Forces in World War II (7 volumes)*, University of Chicago Press 1948-1958

Cole, C, and Cheesman, E F, *The Air Defence of Great Britain, 1914-1918*, London, Puttnam, 1984

Cooper, Malcolm, *The Birth of Independent Air Power*, London, Allen and Unwin, 1986

Dean, Maurice, *The Royal Air Force and two world wars*, London, 1979

Dudgeon, A G, *The luck of the devil*, Shrewsbury, 1985

Escott, Beryl, *Women in Air Force Blue: the Story of Women in the Royal Air Force from 1918 to the Present Day*, Wellingborough, Patrick Stephens, 1989

Frankland, Noble, *Bomber Offensive: The Devastation of Europe*, London, MacDonald, 1970

Franks, N L R, and Bailey, F W, *Over the Front: a complete record of the fighter aces and units of the United States and French air services, 1914-1918,*

London, Grub Street, 1992

Fredette, Raymond H, *The Sky on fire: the First Battle of Britain 1917-1918*, London, Cassell, 1966

Freeman, Roger A, Crouchman, Alan, and Maslen, Vic, *The Mighty Eighth War Diary*, London, Jane's, 1981

Gould, M H, *The Royal Naval Air Service*, Burnham on Crouch, Forces Postal History Society, 1983

Gowing, M, *Independence and Deterrence: Britain and Atomic Energy, 1945-1952*, Volume I: *Policy Making*, Volume II: *Policy Execution*, London, MacMillan, 1974

Grey, C G, *A history of the Air Ministry*, London, 1940

Halley, James J, *The Squadrons of the Royal Air Force and Commonwealth 1918-1988*, London, Air-Britain, 1988

Haslam, E B, *The history of Royal Air Force Cranwell*, London, 1982

Haythornthwaite, Philip, *The World War One Source Book*, London, Cassell, 1992

Hinsley, F Harry et al, *British Intelligence in the Second World War* (6 volumes), London, HMSO, 1979-1990

Hurst, Norman, 'Royal Naval Air Service', *Family Tree Magazine*, January 1994 Vol 10 no 3, pp 8-9

Hyde, H Montgomery, *British aviation policy between the Wars*, London, 1976

James, John, *The paladins: a social history of the RAF up to the outbreak of World War II*, London, 1990

Jones, Neville, *The Origins of Strategic Bombing: A study of British Air Strategic Thought and Practice up to 1918*, London, William Kimber, 1973

Kennett, Lee, *The First Air War 1914-1918*, New York, MacMillan, 1991

Lee, D, *Flight from the Middle East*, London, HMSO, 1980

127

Lee, D, *Eastward: A History of the Royal Air Force in the Far East, 1945-1972*, London, HMSO, 1984

Lee, D, *Wings in the Sun: a History of the Royal Air Force in the Mediterranean, 1945-1986*, London, HMSO, 1989

Lee, David, *Never stop the engine when it's hot*, London, 1983

Lewis, Peter, *British Aircraft 1809-1914*, London, Puttnam, 1962

Middlebrook, Martin, and Everitt, Chris, *The Bomber Command War Diaries*, London, Penguin, 1985

NAPLIB Directory of Aerial Photographic Collections in the United Kingdom 1993, National Association of Photographic Libraries and Information Bureaux, 1993

Old Cranwellian Association, *List of graduates 5 February 1920 - 30 April 1952*, Cranwell, 1952

Omissi, David E, *Air power and colonial control: the Royal Air Force 1919-1939*, Manchester, 1990

Oulton, W, *Christmas Island Cracker: An Account of the Planning and Execution of the British Thermo-Nuclear Bomb Tests, 1957*, Thomas Harmsworth, 1987

Penrose, Harald, *British aviation: the adventuring years 1920-1929*, London, 1973

Penrose, Harald, *British aviation: widening horizons 1930-1934*, London, 1979

Penrose, Harald, *British aviation: the ominous skies 1935-1939*, London, 1980

Pierre, A J, *Nuclear Politics: the British Experience with an Independent Nuclear Force*, Oxford University Press, 1972

Postgate, M, *Operation Firedog: Air Support in the Malayan Emergency, 1948-1960*, London, HMSO, 1992

Probert, Air Cdre Henry, *High Commanders of the Royal Air Force*, London,

HMSO, 1991

Raleigh, Sir Walter, and Jones, H A, *The War in the Air: Being the Story of the Part Played in the Great War by the Royal Air Force* (6 volumes), Oxford University Press, 1922-1937

Richards, Denis, and Saunders, Hilary St George, *Royal Air Force 1939-1945* (3 volumes), London, HMSO, 1953-1954

Roskill, Capt S W, *Documents relating to the Naval Air Service*, Volume 1: *1908-1918*, Naval Records Society, vol 113, 1969

Roskill, Capt S W, *Naval Policy between the Wars*, London, Collins, 1968-1976

Shores, Christopher, Franks, Norman, and Guest, Russell, *Above the Trenches: a complete record of the Fighter Aces and Units of the British Empire Air Forces, 1915-1920*, London, Grub Street, 1990

Smith, Malcolm, *British air strategy between the Wars*, Oxford, 1984

Sturtivant, Ray, *The Squadrons of the Fleet Air Arm*, London, Air-Britain, 1984

Sturtivant, Ray, *Royal Naval Aircraft Serials and Numbers*, London, Air-Britain, 1990

Tavender, I T, *The Distinguished Flying Medal: a record of courage 1918-1982*, Polstead, 1990

Thetford, Owen, *British Royal Aircraft since 1912*, London, Puttnam, 1982

Thetford, Owen, *Aircraft of the Royal Air Force since 1918*, London, Puttnam, 1988

Thompson, Sir Robert, *The Royal Flying Corps*, London, Hamish Hamilton, 1968

Till, G, *Air Power and the Royal Navy, 1914-1945: An Historical Survey*, London, Jane's, 1979

Walker, Percy B, *Early Aviation at Farnborough, Volume 1: Balloons, Kites and Airships*, London, MacDonald, 1971

Webster, Sir Charles, and Frankland, Noble, *The Strategic Air Offensive against Germany, 1939-1945* (4 volumes), London, HMSO, 1961

Wheeler, Allen, *Flying between the Wars*, Henley-on-Thames, 1972

Willis, Steve, and Holliss, Barry, *Military Airfields in the British Isles 1939-1945*, Newport Pagnell, Enthusiasts Publications, 1989

Index

A

B

E

East Africa, RNAS in, 13
Eastern Air Command, 61
Economic Warfare, Ministry of, 58
Egypt, 13, 98
    Air Liaison Mission, 61
    Flying Training School, 33

F

Falklands War, 124
Far East, 94
    Air Force Commands, 95
    photographs, 65
    PoWs in, 70
    War Cabinet Committees, 53
Farnborough *see* Royal Aircraft Establishment;
    Royal Aircraft Factory
Ferry Command, 45, 60, 62
    Atlantic Ferry Organization (ATFERO), 45,
      60
    see also Transport Command
Fighter Command, 38, 45, 58, 59, 62, 67, 69, 94
    narratives, 38
Fighter Establishment, Central, 74, 93
Films, 40
Fleet Air Arm, xi, 38, 67, 106-111
    Combat Reports, 67, 108, 109
    history, 106-109
    in Korea, 109
    Museum, 110
    Position Codes, 64
    records of service, 110
    technical developments, 110
Flying Log Books, 67
Flying Personnel Research Committee, 73
Foreign Office
    aviation abroad, 18
France
    air services, 18
    aircraft, 18
    Anglo-French Committees, War Cabinet, 53
    Army in, 6
    British Air Forces in, 60
    British aircraft sent to, 15
    British Expeditionary Force, 3
    deaths in, 21
    Indochina, 88
    operations, 18, 59
    RFC in, 6, 21

G

Gallipoli, RNAS in, 13
Gas Turbine Establishment, National, 75, 123
    see also Jet development
Germany
    air force, 54, 66, 121
    air raids by, 11, 12
    air raids on, 5, 7, 11
    aircraft

        captured, 18
        crashed, 69
        industry, 2
        messages dropped by, 22
        photographs, 123
        surrender and disposal, 89
    airships, 16, 18
    bombing of, 57, 66
    British Air Forces of Occupation (BAFO),
      88, 89
    captured documents, 40
    East Africa, 13
    local time, 64
    personnel, 18
    photographs, 65, 124
    PoW camps, 69, 70
    PoWs, interrogated, 18
    U Boats, 25
    see also Berlin Airlift; Zeppelins
Gibraltar, 58, 60, 62
Gliders, 75
Graves, 22
    see also Commonwealth War Graves
      Commission
Greenwich Mean Time
    calculating, 63, 64
Groups, 76
    BAFO, 89
    ORBs, 62, 65
    orders, 8
Gulf War, 124

H

Histories *see* Official Histories
Holland, 59
    photographs, 65
    PoW camps, 70
    relief food supplies for, 61
Home Commands
    chart of, 45
    ORBs, 38
Hospitals, 76
    records, 22

I

IAF *see* Independent Air Force
Iceland, 58, 60
Imperial War Museum, 40
Independent Air Force (IAF), 41, 124
    bombing, 11
    establishment, 7
India, 30, 37, 41, 42
    medals, 31
    Overseas Commands, 59
    Sir John Salmond report, 37
Indonesian 'Confrontation', 86, 99, 100
Intelligence, 65, 66
    Directorate of, 65, 66, 69, 123
    photographic, 65, 123
    PoW camps, 70

reports, RNAS, 9
Operations Record Books (ORBs), 9, 35, 61-65, 94-96
    Aircraft Torpedo Development Unit, 34
    Armoured Car Companies, 37
    Commands, 38, 62
    Fleet Air Arm, 107
    Groups, 62
    Home Commands, 38
    Korean War, 96, 97, 102
    Miscellaneous Units, 64
    Overseas Commands, 38, 62
    Squadrons *see* Squadrons
    Stations, 35, 36, 52, 64, 65, 68, 122
    Suez, 99
    WAAF, 66
    Wings, 62, 65
ORBs *see* Operations Record Books
Orders of Battle, 10
Overseas Commands, 38, 53, 59, 60, 65
    demobilization, 87, 88

P

Palestine Brigade, RFC, 13
Palestine Campaign, 13, 123
    RAF Armoured Car Companies, 36
Parachutes, 75
Persia, operations in, 14
Personal reminiscences
    early, 15
    RAF officers, 21, 33
    RFC, 20
Personnel Management Centre, 102
Photographic intelligence, 65
Photographic Interpretation Units, 122, 123
    photo-interpreters, 67
Photographic reconnaissance, 10, 62
Photographic Reconnaissance Unit, 58, 122
Photographs, 15, 40, 41, 121-125
    aerial, 10
    air raids, 12
    aircraft, 16, 123
    airfields, 17, 71
    airships, 25, 122, 123
        German, 18
    airship sheds, 17, 18, 25, 36
    balloons, 122, 123
    Gallipoli, 13
    hangars, 36
    Italy, 13, 65, 123
    Mesopotamia, 13
    Middle East, 123
    in ORBs, 122
    Palestine Campaign, 13, 123
    pilots, 19
    PMRAFNS, 32
    PoW camps, 70
    RAF Stations, 71
    seaplane bases, 17
    Western Front, 10, 17
    in Whittle papers, 73

Pilots, 18, 119
    combat reports, 10, 67
    deaths, 22
    logbooks, 10, 39, 67
    nominal roll, 1914, 21
    reminiscences, 21
    see also Training
PMRAFNS *see* Princess Mary's Royal Air Force
    Nursing Service
Poland, 65
Power Jets Ltd, 71, 73, 74
Princess Mary's Royal Air Force Nursing Service
    (PMRAFNS), 32, 46, 47, 49
Prisoner of war camps, 69, 70
Prisoners of war (PoWs), 23, 54, 69, 70
    British, 23, 69, 70, 82
        escapes, 61
    Dominion Air Force, 70, 82
    German, 18
Propaganda leaflets, 12, 40

R

Radar, 55, 72
    Central Fighter Establishment,
        74, 93
    development, 34
    see also Royal Radar Establishment
RAE *see* Royal Aircraft Establishment
RAF *see* Royal Air Force
Reconnaissance, 10, 11, 65
    balloon, 10
    reports, 11
    Squadrons, USAAF, 122
Remembrance, Book of, 79, 80, 82
Research examples
    bombing operation, 77, 78
    Brown, Capt A Roy, 25, 26
    life of an aircraft, 79, 80
    Red Baron, 25, 26
    Rigid Airship No 9, 25
    Roll of Honour, 79
Reserve, 32, 33
RFC *see* Royal Flying Corps
RNAS *see* Royal Naval Air Service
Rocket Propulsion Establishment, 75
Roll of Honour, 21, 79-82
Royal Aero Club, aviation certificates, 19, 21
Royal Air Force, 5, 6
    communiqués, 9
    establishment, 5-7
    expansion, 38
    Inspectorate General, 61
    manpower policy, 100, 101
    officers, 20, 46, 47
    official history, 24
    organization, 8, 38
    ranks, 46-49
    weekly locations, 10
    weekly orders, 8
Royal Air Force Museum, 40
    records held by, 9, 16, 18, 19, 22, 31-40, 67,
        69, 94, 124